Haunted Indiana

Haunted Indiana

Ghosts and Strange Phenomena of the Hoosier State

James A. Willis
Illustrations by Marc Radle

STACKPOLE
BOOKS

Published by
STACKPOLE BOOKS
5067 Ritter Road
Mechanicsburg, PA 17055
www.stackpolebooks.com

Printed in the United States of America

10 9 8 7 6 5 4 3 2 1

FIRST EDITION

Cover design by Tessa J. Sweigert

This book is intended as entertainment and as a historical record of ghost stories, legends, and folklore from Indiana. Many of these stories cannot be independently confirmed or corroborated, and the author and publisher make no representation as to their factual accuracy. Readers should be advised that some of the sites described in this book are located on private property and should not be visited, or they may face prosecution for trespassing.

Library of Congress Cataloging-in-Publication Data

Willis, James A.
    Haunted Indiana : ghosts and strange phenomena of the Hoosier State / James A. Willis ; illustrations by Marc Radle. — 1st ed.
        p. cm.
    Includes bibliographical references (p.   ).
    ISBN 978-0-8117-0779-4 (pbk.)
    1. Haunted places—Indiana. 2. Ghosts—Indiana. I. Title.
    BF1472.U6W5553 2012
    133.109772—dc23
                                                    2011040272

To Courtney
For allowing me to be the center of her universe,
if only for a while

Contents

Contents

Introduction

SO HOW DOES A GUY WHO'S SPENT THE LAST TWELVE YEARS CHASING after ghosts in Ohio end up writing a book about Indiana hauntings? Guess you could call it destiny. You see, for years now, whenever my travels took me to the western part of Ohio, I'd always know when I was close to the Indiana border. Things just started to feel weird. It wasn't anything you could put your finger on. It was as if all these strange and spooky ghosts and creatures were standing on the other side of the imaginary borderline, daring me to cross over and try to find them.

In late 2007, the two "Weird" Marks, Mark Moran and Mark Sceurman, tapped me to help out on the book *Weird Indiana* with Troy Taylor and Mark Merriman. Suddenly, I had carte blanche and permission to step over the border and explore Indiana. And let me tell you, the state didn't let me down.

Sure, the state had plenty of traditional urban legends—tales such as Bloody Mary and the Vanishing Hitchhiker. But there was so much more. Having now worked on books chronicling ghost stories for many different states, I can honestly tell you that Indiana has some of the most disturbing and twisted ghost stories in existence. What other state can claim a creature that is half woman and half dog makes its home there? Or have a bridge that's haunted by a ghostly purple head? And of course, leave it to Indiana to give one of the creepiest places in the state the grin-inducing nickname Okie Pinokie.

I also noticed something else as I trekked across the wonderful state of Indiana. Mainly, that the state is very reluctant to give up its ghost stories. I have been to many states where people are literally falling over each other to tell me their ghostly tales. No so with Indiana. They keep their stories close to the vest, which makes it all the more satisfying when they finally give up the ghost (literally) and let you in on their spectral secrets. Then and only then do you realize that these tales have been around for years, many being handed down from generation to generation. Sure, some of the tales leave you scratching your head and wondering aloud, "could something like that really happen?" But really, that's not the allure of Indiana's ghost stories. Rather, it's how they have become entwined with actual history to give the state of Indiana a truly rich tapestry of folklore. That's where the mystique of these stories lies. And really, would we expect anything from a state whose very nickname—the Hoosier State—is steeped in mystery and folklore?

So come with me now, if you dare, on a strange and spooky journey across Indiana. We'll take a trip over some haunted bridges, pass a few spooky houses, try to explain why Indiana has so many ghosts associated with the color blue, and just for fun, stroll on over to Hell's Gate. Along the way, we'll encounter a few ghosts and even some hideous beasts. This trip will be unlike any other you've ever taken. Enjoy the ride!

South Bend
and
Northern Indiana

FAR AND AWAY, THE HIGHEST CONCENTRATION OF INDIANA GHOST STORIES is in the northern part of the state. This may have something to do with the fact that from the very beginning, people in northern Indiana just seemed to like sharing and trading things.

In the 1600s, some of the first people to cross into what is now Indiana were French fur traders from Canada, who brought with them items from Europe to trade with the Native American tribes there. To further spread their business, these traders plied the waters around Indiana, especially Lake Michigan and the St. Joseph River. They created a large trading post at the river's southernmost bend. That little trading post eventually grew into a city, and its location along the St. Joseph inspired its name: South Bend.

Some four hundred years later, that same trading spirit lives on among the people of Northern Indiana. Only now, they are trading ghost stories. As I noted in the introduction, Hoosiers tend to keep quiet when it comes to their ghostlore, but this is not so in Northern Indiana. Rather, they seem to delight in sharing their stories.

Throwing Coins through the Cemetery Fence

Anyone who has traveled down the rural roads of Northern Indiana for any length of time gets used to all sorts of things popping up in front of his or her car—deer, raccoons, and even the occasional discarded fast-food wrapper. But take a trip down 5th Road in Bremen and be prepared for the shock of a lifetime when it suddenly looks like you're going to drive smack-dab into the middle of a cemetery—a haunted one to boot!

The graveyard in question is Ewald Cemetery. Although a series of ninety-degree turns will take you out of harm's way and allow you to continue on your journey, it is nonetheless a bit unsettling to see a cemetery looming in your headlights. Perhaps that's why people started saying that something wasn't right out there. Of course, that doesn't explain why to this day, the cemetery is widely known as Little Egypt.

Although there are several reported ghosts at the cemetery, most of the tales center around those of little children. One of the most popular stories says that if you throw a penny or a nickel on top of a child's grave, you will hear a ghostly cry. This is easier said than done, however. Not only is the cemetery surrounded by a fence that is usually locked, but many of the old stones have unfortunately been vandalized, making it nearly impossible to determine which of the graves belong to children. Still, it is not uncommon to stop by the cemetery and see coins scattered around the grounds, because people throw them over the fence toward random plots as if they were playing a game of chance at a carnival.

Another story says that while you might not actually see a ghost while you are at the cemetery, you will see signs that they were present. Some people have reported that after walking around the fence of the cemetery for a while and returning to their cars, they have found dozens of tiny handprints all over their vehicles, almost as if a group of children had been playing around them.

There is also a story about the field in which the cemetery is situated. Those who foolishly visit late at night are often frightened off by the ghostly apparition of a man who emerges from the field and walks towards them. Some believe that this is the ghost of a former caretaker, still watching over the cemetery. Others, though, say the man is a farmer who was murdered in the field, which he used to own.

A final bizarre tale concerns a bridge that is a short distance east of the cemetery. The bridge that crosses the Yellow River is referred to as the Troll Bridge, and it is said that a giant, eight-foot creature lives there. He, or it, has been reported to come rushing out from under the bridge at those who approach it, and it chases them, even after they've returned to their cars and hightailed it out of there.

So are there stories true? It's hard to say with any certainty. But ask anyone who has traveled down 5th Road in the middle of the night and they'll tell you there's definitely something spooky going on there.

What Goes Up Must Be Getting Pushed by Ghostly Hands

When it comes to the subject of ghosts, there are several theories as to why some spirits make the decision to linger here on Earth. Some ghosts are said to be lost; others are plain stubborn. Some decide to hang around so they can remain with friends and loved ones. And some just want to make sure what happened to them doesn't happen to anyone else. The latter may be the reason why a group of ghostly schoolchildren are said to have taken up residence at the site of their demise more than forty years ago.

Classic ghost stories have never been big on specifics, and the case of the tale surrounding the hill on County Line Road in Westville is no exception. All that is said is that sometime in the 1960s, there was a set of railroad tracks at the bottom of this hill. One fateful day, a busload of children somehow managed to get stuck on the tracks. Worse, there was a train coming. Try as he might, the bus driver was unable to move the bus off the tracks and the train hit it at a high rate of speed, killing all of the children and the driver instantly.

After such a horrible accident, the area residents wanted to forget it ever happened as soon as possible, so they had the train tracks removed. Once that was accomplished, everyone put the incident behind them and moved on with their lives, forgetting that it ever happened. Everyone, that is, except for the ghosts of the children who died in the wreck.

According to legend, the ghostly schoolchildren still hang around the area of the crash, even after all these years. What's more, they go to great lengths to ensure no one suffers the same fate they did. That's why, even though the train tracks are long gone, people who park their cars on the spot of the accident find their vehicles being pushed away and slowly up the nearby hill. Some people are said to have gone so far as to sprinkle flour all over the bumpers of their cars, so that they can see the tiny hand-prints of the ghostly children who push their vehicles.

The Great Circus Train Disaster

In the early part of the twentieth century, the Hagenbeck-Wallace Circus of Peru, Indiana, was one of the most popular in the United States, second only to Ringling Brothers. By crating up equipment, performers, and animals into boxcars, the circus was able to use the railroad to travel the country, bringing happiness and joy wherever it went. Sadly, those very rails caused the worst circus train wreck in U.S. history.

In the early morning hours of June 22, 1918, a train with everything needed to move the entire circus, including fourteen flatcars, seven stock cars to house the animals, and four sleeper cars, was barreling across Indiana toward the town of Hammond, where the circus was scheduled to give a performance in the coming days. As the train passed through the town of Ivanhoe, conductor R. W. Johnson thought he smelled smoke. Believing the train was over-heating, he ordered the engineer to stop. Once the train had come to a complete halt at a crossing known as Ivanhoe Interlocking, per standard operating procedures, Johnson dispatched a flagman to the rear of the train to keep an eye on things while he checked for the source of the smoke.

As Johnson inspected the train, he was unaware that miles down the track disaster was heading his way in the form of Engine Number 8485. Operated by engineer Alonzo K. Sargent, this empty Michigan Central Railroad troop train had left Kalamazoo, Michigan, and was now pulling twenty empty Pullman cars to Chicago.

To make matters worse, Sargent would later testify that he had taken several "kidney pills" earlier in the evening that made him drowsy. In truth, Sargent was falling asleep at the controls as the train rolled on at speeds upwards of thirty-five miles per hour. Sargent claimed he never saw any warning signs or even a flagman and he didn't know anything was wrong until almost the moment of impact.

The flagman who had been stationed at the back of the circus train stated that he tried in vain to get the oncoming engine to slow down. At a few minutes past 4:00 A.M., the flagman watched helplessly as the troop train slammed into the back of the circus train. Upon impact, several of the circus cars burst into flame. The flames immediately began to spread through the cars, no doubt fueled by the many kerosene lanterns inside the train. Of course, the fact that all of the cars were made of wood didn't help matters either. Before long, the entire circus train was fully engulfed, swallowing up both man and beast. Those who were able to escape the blaze tried valiantly to save those who were still trapped inside. But since they were still more than five miles away from the nearest town, Hammond, there was little they could do but watch the train burn and try to cover their ears to block out the horrible cries of humans and animals being burned alive.

When the flames were finally extinguished around 8:00 A.M., the overwhelming task of trying to identify the dead and help the injured began. One look at the scene was all officials needed to know that they had their work cut out for them. Many of the bodies were burned beyond recognition, and in some cases, a single limb was all that remained of an individual. Still others completely burned away, essentially vanishing from the crash scene. Of the estimated 300 passengers on the train at the time of the collision, 86 were killed and more than 120 others were injured. That does not include the animals, many of which also perished.

Five days after the crash, the remains of between 56 and 61 individuals were taken to Showman's Rest, a 750-acre section of Woodlawn Cemetery in Forest Park, Illinois, and laid to rest. Guarded by five elephant statues, the grave markers there are a stark reminder of the horrible accident. Many of the stones simply read "unknown male" or "unknown female."

So is it any wonder that such a tragic disaster would somehow leave behind a psychic imprint? That's what they say happened as a result of the Hagenbeck-Wallace Circus train wreck. Although it happened almost one hundred years ago, people visiting the site of the crash say they are overcome with a sense of sadness, while others report hearing the sounds of crying and sobbing. And those night owls who have staged an early-morning vigil on the anniversary of the accident claim to have entered some sort of weird time warp where the accident plays itself out in front of them, complete with disembodied screams, the smell of smoke, and even the cries of panicked animals.

Win One for the Gipper . . . and His Ghost, Too!

He is arguably one of the greatest football players to ever play for the Fighting Irish of Notre Dame. His dying words were turned into a motivational speech and were later used as a slogan for a political campaign. With such an illustrious career, is it any wonder that even the ghost of George Gipp is famous?

Born on February 18, 1895, in Laurium, Michigan, George Gipp excelled at sports from an early age. Once accepted at Notre Dame, Gipp originally intended to play for the university's baseball team. Legendary football coach Knute Rockne, however, had other plans for Gipp. Upon seeing him idly tossing a football around, Rockne managed to convince Gipp to play football for him.

Clearly, Rockne saw something in Gipp that no one else did. Despite the fact that Gipp had no experience playing organized football, he quickly excelled at all aspects of the game. Although he was primarily a halfback, he set several records on both offense and defense in the years he played for the Fighting Irish from 1917 to 1920. Gipp is, in fact, still Notre Dame's all-time leader in several categories, including total offense per game.

In December 1920, Gipp came down with pneumonia and was admitted to the hospital. Despite valiant efforts by doctors, his condition worsened to the point that it was clear he would never leave the hospital. Several days later, according to legend, Rockne came to visit Gipp in the hospital. It was during this visit that Gipp is alleged to have uttered the following immortal words: "I've got to go, Rock. It's all right. I'm not afraid. Some time, Rock, when the team is up against it, when things are wrong and the breaks are beating the boys, ask them to go in there with all they've got and win just one for the Gipper."

George Gipp passed away several days later on December 14, 1920. He was only twenty-five years old. Rockne kept the words to Gipp's famous last speech under wraps until November 12, 1928, at Yankee Stadium. It was during halftime, with Notre Dame losing to Army, that Rockne delivered Gipp's words to the team. So inspired was the team that they came back to beat Army 12-6, with Irish player Jack Chevigny reportedly shouting "there's one for the Gipper" as he scored the winning touchdown. Ever since then, the phrase "win just one for the Gipper" has been used to rally people to overcome insurmountable odds.

The speech would also figure prominently in the 1940 movie *Knute Rockne, All American*, with Ronald Reagan playing the role of George Gipp. Reagan would come to be nicknamed "the Gipper" for the rest of his life, going so far as to incorporate parts of Gipp's famous speech into his successful presidential campaign.

Having lived such a successful and fabled life, Gipp might choose to return to literally dozens of places. Washington Hall, Notre Dame's campus theater, probably wouldn't be on that list, though. And yet, that's where his ghost is said to appear. There is a long-standing rumor concerning Washington Hall and just how Gipp came down with his fatal pneumonia. As the story goes, Gipp would sometimes stay out after curfew, often returning to find his dorm room locked up for the night. Rather than risk getting caught trying to sneak back in the dorm, Gipp would head over to Washington Hall because the doors were almost always left unlocked all night. He would then go inside and sleep in the theater. On a fateful night in December 1920, according to legend, Gipp returned to campus to find himself locked out of the dorm. Unfortunately, Washington Hall was also locked up that night, forcing Gipp to sleep on the steps of the building. This, they say, is how Gipp contracted pneumonia.

As for Gipp's ghost, it is very rarely seen inside the hall. It instead decides to make its presence known by knocking on walls, opening and closing doors, and generally making strange sounds in the dead of night. When Gipp's ghost does decide to make an appearance, however, it does so in style. In the 1920s, Pio Montenegro was living in the Science Hall, which faces Washington Hall. On more than one occasion, Montengro claimed to have looked over from Science Hall and watched as a ghostly white horse and rider galloped up the steps of Washington Hall. The ghostly rider? None other than George Gipp himself!

Elizabeth, the Hitchhiking Ghost

Perhaps one of the most popular Indiana ghost stories concerns a stretch of Reeder Road between Merrillville and Griffith. It involves a woman named Elizabeth and an event that happened on the road in 1955.

According to legend, Elizabeth was driving home one dark night. As she traveled down Reeder Road, she lost control of her car and crashed into a swamp. Try as she might, Elizabeth was unable to free herself from the car and she drowned. After her body was recovered, her family had her buried in nearby Ross Cemetery. Most thought that was the end of the story, but it was only the beginning. That's because, shortly after the funeral, people began to report seeing Elizabeth's ghost standing alongside Reeder Road near the spot of her fatal car accident.

These tales at first were dismissed as being the work of overactive imaginations. But then the stories took an ever stranger twist. On certain nights, Elizabeth's ghost was not only appearing, but it was also accepting rides. Numerous people stepped forward to say that while driving down Reeder Road at night, they had encountered a pale young girl, standing all alone along the road. Thinking the girl needed help, they pulled over and offered her a ride, which she accepted. After telling these good Samaritans that her car had gone off the road and she needed to get home, the girl would climb into the backseat of the car. In some instances, the girl engaged in conversation with the driver, and in others, she simply directed them down the road toward her house. But in all instances, the girl suddenly and mysteriously vanished from the backseat of the vehicle before reaching Ross Cemetery . . . and while the car was still moving!

Creepiness on Cline Avenue

It is said that sometime in the 1930s, a woman wearing a long white dress was driving down Cline Avenue in Gary with several of her children in the car with her. As she approached the intersection of Cline and 5th Avenues, she was involved in an accident that took the lives of the children. Shortly after the funerals, the woman returned to the scene of the accident and took to walking up and down Cline Avenue, apparently mourning the loss of her children. Eventually, the woman went mad and finally committed suicide.

There are those who claim that on certain nights, the woman's ghost, wearing the long, white dress, returns to the scene of the accident and wanders up and down Cline Avenue in search of her children. Others do not see the strange woman, but have reported hearing disembodied moaning and crying.

A second version of this story exists. In this one, the woman gets in the witnesses' car! According to this story, there once was a beautiful young woman who fell in love with a man of whom her family didn't approve. So the couple often met in secret down near the banks of the Calumet River. The couple eventually decided they could no longer be apart and made secret plans to marry at the nearby Catholic church, even going so far as to get the local priest to agree to preside over the clandestine ceremony.

On the day of the wedding, the bride quietly got into her gown and made her way to the church, where she waited for her man. He never showed up. Distraught, the woman, still in her wedding dress, hailed a cab and made her way back home. As the cab traveled along the Calumet River, the woman was so overcome with emotion that she jumped from the moving vehicle and threw herself into the river. Her body was recovered the next day. The woman's final resting place is unknown because at the time Catholic churches did not allow those who had taken their own lives to be buried in their cemeteries. Perhaps this is why the ghost of the young woman returns to the spot where she chose to end her young life, sometimes even hailing a cab in a futile attempt to return home one last time.

The Gypsies' Curse

Some people will tell you that a really good ghost story should not to let the truth get in the way. Such is the case with the story associated with the South East Grove Cemetery in Crown Point.

The long-standing legend concerns a group of Gypsies who supposedly came through the area in the early 1800s. In the most popular version of the legend, the cemetery was not yet in existence when the Gypsies decided to set up camp on the site. They were only there a short period of time before influenza swept through the camp. With nowhere else to turn, the Gypsies reached out to the locals for help. Not only did their cries for help and medicine fall on deaf ears, but the Gypsies were told that they were no longer welcome in the area and were ordered to vacate their camp immediately. The Gypsies pleaded, saying that many of their people were sick or dying and unable to travel, but it was to no avail. Angered at being turned out, the Gypsies departed, but not before they buried their dead at the campsite. In another version of the legend that has the cemetery already in existence, the Gypsies secretly bury their dead at the rear of the graveyard. In both versions, however, the Gypsies put a curse on the land before departing.

The problem with the legend is that there is no record of there ever having been a campsite in the area of South East Grove Cemetery, either before or after the cemetery was established. On top of that, there is nothing to suggest that there are unmarked graves at the back of the cemetery grounds. Still, enough unexplained activity has been reported here to make one wonder if there really might be a curse in effect. For one thing, people have reported weird, bright lights moving throughout the cemetery late at night. There are also strange cold spots that seem to envelop people who visit the grounds, even in the middle of bright sunny days. But by far the weirdest part of the legend says that if you walk around the cursed part of the cemetery, you will find your shoes and the bottoms of your pants covered in a blood-like substance when you return home.

World's Largest Ghost Hunt

With today's plethora of ghost reality shows, ghost hunts have become all the rage. Most states, including Indiana, have locations that for a price offer people the chance to conduct their own overnight ghost hunts. But that wasn't always the case. Many Hoosiers are surprised to find that back in 1965, a small stretch of road in northwest Indiana was home to what has become known as the world's largest ghost hunt.

If you're heading north out of Valparaiso towards Chesterton, you will more than likely find yourself on Campbell Street. It's here, many years before the road was put in, that our story begins. It is said that the local schoolteacher, Annabel, lived here with her husband and their infant son. Unfortunately, Annabel's husband, who had always had something of a temper, had become worse once their son was born. He was now lashing out at Annabel, including abusing her physically.

Fearing for the safety of both herself and her son, Annabel secretly made the decision to leave her husband. One cold winter evening, she waited for her husband to fall asleep and then wrapped up her baby son and snuck out the front door, heading towards town on foot. Suddenly, a freak winter snowstorm blew up, making it nearly impossible for Annabel to see where she was going. As she held her son closer to her for warmth, she didn't realize that she had changed direction and was no longer walking towards town. In fact, she was heading deeper and deeper into the woods. Try as she might, Annabel could not find her way. Eventually, the mother and son perished in the storm. Several days later, the still-frozen bodies were found in the woods.

Almost immediately after Annabel's passing, there were reports of her ghost appearing in the woods, but because the location of her death was in a fairly isolated and wooded area, few people ever ventured out there. All that changed years later when Campbell Street was created, with a portion cut very close to the spot where Annabel and the baby expired.

Soon, reports poured in of a young woman standing at the edge of the woods near the side of Campbell Street. In most cases, the ghost just stood there silently, but sometimes it appeared to be beckoning people to come closer, as if she was asking for help. For the next several years, the ghost story of Annabel remained popular, but only among the locals.

For whatever reason, all that changed in October 1965. It started innocently enough with a couple of local high school students sharing the story with some classmates who were unfamiliar with it. But then some classmates decided to add to the story and claimed to have actually seen Annabel's ghost recently. Before long, interest in the story had been rekindled and began to spread like wildfire. Soon, all the high schools between Valparaiso and Chesterton were abuzz with the story, while dozens of curious students began making plans for late-night trips out to Campbell Street. Even the parents of the high school students, who had grown up with the story, took a renewed interest in the tale. Before long, as night fell on Campbell Street, it became clogged with cars crawling along in the darkness, filled with faces pressed against the windows, hoping to see a ghost.

As Halloween drew closer, the decision was made that something had to be done to curb the amount of people cruising up and down Campbell Street. So the Indiana State Police were called in and did their best to keep things flowing.

It is said that thousands of people visited Campbell Street that October with the hopes of seeing the ghost, but Annabel failed to show up. Perhaps, just like some people, ghosts can be frightened off by crowds. Whatever the case may be, later in the 1970s, the BBC ran on segment about the event, calling it the "World's Largest Ghost Hunt." Unofficially, it remains the largest one to date.

The Water Nymph of Lake Michigan

Take a quick look over any book of ghost stories and you will find that ghosts have been known to wear all sorts of clothing, from rags to ball gowns and military uniforms. The ghost known as Diana of the Dunes, however, is one of the most unique in all of ghostlore: She is almost always seen totally naked!

The woman who would become known as Diana of the Dunes was born Alice Mable Gray in 1881 in Chicago. While little is known about her upbringing, it has been established that Alice was a very intelligent, driven young woman, who graduated with honors from the University of Chicago. At some point around 1915, Alice decided to throw everything away and take up a simpler way of living in the area now known as Dunes State Park in Chesterton. Her exact reason for picking the area is unknown, although there is some speculation that she may have visited the area with her parents as a child. Whatever the reason, the area that Alice chose to live in was a much different place than it is today. Back in 1915, the Dunes was a desolate place that was essentially uninhabited. In fact, Alice later wrote that she slept out on the dunes for several nights until she came upon a house, which was nothing more than an old abandoned shack in which she could take up residence. She had with her nothing more than some simple necessities: two guns and a blanket.

The first "sighting" of Diana of the Dunes came in the spring of 1916, when a fisherman went by a cabin he thought was abandoned and was shocked to see a naked woman swimming in nearby Lake Michigan. After returning to town and telling a few friends what he had seen, the word quickly spread of a "water nymph" frolicking naked in the lake. Before long, local news reporters were headed out to the Dunes to try and track this woman down.

Initially, Alice hid from the reporters. After all, she had come to the Dunes seeking solace and isolation. Hounding reporters was the last thing she wanted to deal with. Eventually, though, she gave in and granted an interview to a reporter from the *Chicago Examiner*. Once that story hit the newswire, it quickly spread, with other reporters adding their own flowery and exaggerated language to the tale. And suddenly, Alice was now Diana of the Dunes. No explanation has been given for the "Diana" moniker; perhaps it just sounded good.

As the news of Diana spread, more and more people came to the dunes hoping to see the now-famous woman. Diana did her best to be polite, but she clearly wanted to be alone. That's why everyone was caught a bit by surprise when around 1921 she began to be seen in the company of a local drifter named Paul Wilson.

The couple remained together for several years, and by most accounts, the relationship was very volatile. It was reported that Wilson often beat Diana. One thing is for certain: once she met Wilson, Diana's desire for a quiet, simple life was over. During their relationship, the pair was accused of burglarizing a home, and they were even involved in a physical confrontation with another man, resulting in Diana having her skull fractured.

Alice Gray died on February 11, 1926, from what is described as uremic poisoning. Of course, word quickly spread that the poisoning was the result of yet another beating at the hands of Wilson. True or not, Wilson didn't get any bonus points by opting to have her remains buried in Oak Lawn Cemetery in Gary. It was believed that Alice wanted to either be buried in her family's plot in Illinois or else be cremated and have her ashes spread across the dunes she had come to know and love. The sad fact is that Alice's final resting place ended up being an unmarked grave in a pauper's field in Oak Lawn Cemetery.

Perhaps that's the reason why, even today, people report seeing the naked ghost of Alice Gray playing in the waters of Lake Michigan and walking slowly among the dunes. Maybe she felt the need to go back to the simple way of life that she had so craved when she was alive.

As If You Needed a Reason to Stay Away from Dog Face Bridge

When walking down the dirt trail through the woods at the end of S County Road 1100 West, just outside of San Pierre, it's hard to believe that you are treading on what used to be a road and that two bridges used to stand here. The first bridge is still visible in the underbrush, but the second is all but gone now. It's at this second bridge that people are said to have encountered one of the strangest beings in all of Indiana, if not the United States. What is it? A ghost? A monster? Well, whatever it is, one thing is for certain: if you see it, you better get out of its way!

The story that gave birth to this creature begins in the 1950s with a young woman driving down S County Road 1100 West alone at night (in more recent versions of the tale, the woman is a passenger and a male companion is driving). The woman makes it across the first bridge without incident, but just as she is preparing to cross the second bridge, a large dog runs out into the road. The woman swerves in a vain attempt to miss the dog, causing her to

lose control of the car and crash into the side of the bridge. The woman and the dog are both killed instantly.

It must have been a horrible wreck, for when rescue workers arrived, they found that both the woman and the dog had been decapitated. Worse, the woman's body and the dog's head were missing. They were never recovered.

Late-night visitors to the bridges have stated that as soon as they cross over the first bridge, they are immediately overcome with the feeling that they are not alone. Those brave enough to continue down the path report hearing strange growling noises coming from the woods around them and seeing glowing eyes peering back at them. Doglike whines and cries are also commonly heard. But that is nothing compared to what awaits you at the second bridge.

It is said that upon reaching the remains of the second bridge, you will be confronted by the hideous sight of a creature with the head of a dog and the body of a woman. Needless to say, this beast is never in the best of moods, and if it sees you, it will let out a shriek and come at you. At this point, it would be best if you beat a hasty retreat back to your car, because if it manages to catch you, you can be fairly certain that it's not going to be pretty!

The Osceola Poltergeist

With a total area of little under one-and-a-half square miles, it would be safe to say that nothing too exciting happens in the tiny town of Osceola in St. Joseph County. And yet, one event occurred here in 1966 that literally got things flying!

One September night of that year, a husband returned home with his wife and young son to find their Greenlawn Avenue house a mess. Items had been thrown from shelves and furniture had been tipped over and moved about the room. Initially, believing they had just been robbed, the family began moving from room to room to try to determine what exactly had been taken. They were perplexed to find that not a single thing was missing. Next, they checked all the windows and doors to see how the vandal broke into the house. Once again, the family came up empty; all the windows and doors were locked up tight. Scratching their heads, the family decided to just forget the whole thing, and after cleaning up the house, they went to bed.

Things went on as usual at the house for the next few days. But then, suddenly, furniture started sliding across the floor and household items fell from the shelves, this time in full view of the family. With nowhere else to turn, they decided to call the police. When the St. Joseph County sheriff arrived at the house, he, too, was witness to objects moving around. The sheriff even went so far as to file an official police report, even though he was unable to determine the cause of the strange activity taking place at the house.

As the sheriff left the house, he couldn't stop thinking about what he had just witnessed. Seeking answers, he reached out to the University of Notre Dame and even invited several professors from a range of disciplines to look into the case. It was at this point, no doubt, that the term "poltergeist" was mentioned. Loosely translated as "noisy ghost" in German, a poltergeist is a specific type of ghost that makes its presence known by moving objects, often violently. There is also a separate school of thought that believes poltergeist activity is usually centered around a young child, especially one nearing puberty. It is thought that the emotional turmoil going on inside a child at that time can attract poltergeists. Whatever the professors might have thought was causing the activity, they, too, were unable to confirm the source for all the ruckus inside the house.

The investigation continued for several more weeks until October 12, 1966, when the St. Joseph County sheriff held a very brief press conference in which he simply stated that all the activity in the house was being caused by the family's young son and that the case was now closed. No further explanation was given, and the sheriff refused to answer any questions after the press conference was over.

Percival, the Phantom of the Opera House

Over the course of its 115-year history, the Bristol Opera House has operated as many different things—an opera house (obviously), a movie theater, and even a skating rink. Indeed, about the only thing that has remained constant at the Bristol is its ghosts.

Built in 1896 by Horace and Cyrus Mosier, the Bristol Opera House was an immediate success, and productions there continually played to packed houses. But as the years went by and people's tastes changed, more and more of the opera house's seats were left empty. By the 1930s, the stage was dark and the building was all but abandoned, in use simply as a storage facility.

In 1960, with the opera house literally crumbling and waiting for its date with the wrecking ball, it was saved by the Elkhart Civic Theatre Company, which leased the building. The theatre company spent the next year fixing up the building and then opened it up the following year, much to the delight of its neighbors and, if the stories are to be believed, the local ghosts.

It is said that renovating a building can revive curious ghosts. Perhaps that's what happened at the opera house, because shortly after the theater company began its renovations, the ghosts came out to play.

The first to make its presence known was the ghost of a man named Percival. As the story goes, when Percival's entire family became homeless after their house burned to the ground, the original owners of the Bristol took pity on them and allowed the family to live in the opera house until they were back on their feet. In exchange for a place to stay, Percival agreed to become the opera house's unofficial handyman, a job he apparently took so seriously that he's still doing it today. Percival's ghost is seen throughout the opera house, making the rounds just to ensure everything is working as it should. He's also said to be quite particular about where tools are placed and has been known to move them around when he's not happy with where they've been left. And Percival is apparently something of a ladies' man; he is often seen in and around the women's dressing room.

Another ghost seen in the theater is nicknamed "Beth" by the actors and actresses who have seen her. Beth is described as a young girl who is usually only seen from the audience and when the curtains are closed. Beth's ghost likes to peek out from behind the curtain and study the seats. She is never seen anywhere else in the theater, although some blame Beth for the unexplained banging and rattling noises that often echo through the building late at night.

A final ghost said to inhabit the opera house is a mysterious figure referred to as "Helen." Although she is described as a "middle-aged woman," very few people have actually seen her. They simply feel her presence, especially directors and producers, to whom Helen is said to take a liking, so much so that she is often referred as their "protector."

Stephanie Cries Out For Help

There's nothing like a walk in a state forest to get your head back on straight. The clean, fresh air. The sounds of nature all around you. The overpowering sense that something horrible is stalking you through the woods. What's that? You're not up for being chased through the forest by something ungodly? Well then, you'd better steer clear of the Frances Slocum State Forest in Peru. Otherwise, you might find yourself smack-dab in the middle of an area of woods known as Okie Pinokie, Indiana's answer to the Blair Witch Woods.

If you go looking for Okie Pinokie on any map, you're going to be disappointed. That's because the name refers to an unmarked area of the Frances Slocum State Forest near County Road 510 East. And while the jury's still out as to where the name Okie Pinokie originated, we do know where the name of the state forest came from. Frances Slocum was a young Quaker girl who was kidnapped from her home in Pennsylvania by the Lenape Indians on November 2, 1778. Some fifty years later, her brothers found her living in New Reserve, Indiana, among the Miami tribe. But that's where history stops and legend takes over.

In order to enter Okie Pinokie, one needs to pass by three stone pillars, park their car at the turnaround, and then follow the path into the woods. Most people are barely out of their cars when they begin to feel as if they are being watched. As they walk deeper and deeper into the woods, that feeling becomes overpowering. They see dark shapes and figures moving around in the trees, but just who or what these figures are is unclear. Some believe they are the departed souls of Native Americans who passed away here or else were buried nearby. Others think the shapes belong to strange dog-like creatures that can be heard growling, barking, or whistling from deep within the woods. Whatever they are, these beings by all accounts are not happy and have been known to chase people back to their cars.

There is also a long-standing rumor that several decomposing bodies have been found tucked away here over the years. Who these people were or who placed their bodies in the state forest has never been determined. So their restless spirits are forced to wander here, hoping for the day when they are finally identified and can rest in peace. In that regard, Okie Pinokie could be considered hell on Earth for those unlucky spirits.

By far, the most disturbing spirit said to haunt Okie Pinokie is a young girl named Stephanie. It is said that Stephanie was brought into these woods and tortured, raped, and murdered by an assailant who was never caught. Legend holds that if you go to a specific spot inside Okie Pinokie and call out for Stephanie, your cries will be answered by the sounds of a young girl screaming in agony and sobbing uncontrollably.

The Seven Pillars

Many, many years ago, as the Mississinewa River made its way south from Peru, Indiana, it started lapping at the limestone cliffs along the riverbed. Slowly, the water started eroding the limestone, creating small pockets. The water continued flowing, and as it did, those pockets formed the cavelike structures that are today known as Seven Pillars.

The Miami Indians knew the moment they first set eyes on Seven Pillars that it was a special location. Some of them may have even believed that within the natural structure was a portal of sorts that would allow them to communicate with their ancestors. So they began to hold their tribal council meetings at Seven Pillars, calling out for the spirits of those who had gone before them to come forth and guide their decision-making process. Whether or not there was an actual portal at Seven Pillars is certainly open to debate. But enough of the local settlers were convinced of the supernatural activity that they avoided the area at all costs. Even when Seven Pillars became a popular trading post because of its convenient location along the river, some took to wearing protective amulets and religious medals to try and keep them safe from any spirit that might be lurking there.

There are also reports that the tribal council held trials at Seven Pillars, with the harshest sentence being death by beheading, which was said to be carried out on the same spot. What became of the bodies, or the heads, for that matter, of those who were put to death is unknown. The legends might account for the reports from local fishermen on the Mississinewa River of seeing dark figures moving among the rocks, even in broad daylight.

Until recently, the area surrounding Seven Pillars was open for overnight camping. Those brave enough to spend the night here were sometimes awakened to find there was something new at the campsite—a ghost. Sometimes the ghost appeared as a ball of bright, glowing light, and at other times it appeared to be a human being that would suddenly vanish.

Ghosts in the Theater Balcony

Officially, Kendallville's Strand Theatre is known as one of the oldest continually operating theaters in the United States. Unofficially, it's also known as one of the most haunted buildings in Kendallville.

The fact that there were several other theaters in Kendallville around the turn of the century didn't deter E. B. Spencer from building his own seven-hundred-seat building on Main Street in 1890. When he was done, Spencer so loved the building that he named it the Spencer Opera House.

The building passed through several owners until Robert Hudson Sr. purchased it in 1928. One year later, he reopened it as the Strand Theatre. Although the Strand was a successful business venture right from the beginning, Hudson was constantly looking for ways to improve it. He eventually expanded the theater to accommodate nearly 950 patrons, all of whom could see the stage from either the main floor or the balcony, which wrapped around the rear of the theater and held the projection room.

When Hudson died in 1972, his wife took over. Several years later, she made the decision to divide the giant theater into two separate ones. She also divided the balcony, so that each of the two theaters had its own balcony. When she was done, one theater seated 222 people on the main level with room for another 82 in the balcony. The other theater accommodated one more person, or 223, on the main floor and 80 in the balcony.

It is the balcony areas of the Strand where the spirits are said to reside, especially near the projection room that straddles the two balconies. The reason for this is, according to a long-standing rumor, a former employee committed suicide in the projection room. His ghost is sometimes seen by patrons and employees alike, standing inside the projection room or on the stairs leading to the balconies. One documented sighting concerned the two small children of a cleaning-crew member who were playing in the theater while their parent was working. Both children reported looking up at the balcony staircase and becoming frightened upon seeing the ghost of a man standing there, staring at them.

Mr. Moody and His Lantern

Ask any paranormal researcher and they will tell you that one of the most frustrating things about their job is that ghosts won't perform on cue. Many times, ghost hunters will spend hours at a location, only to come away empty-handed. If you're one of those people who don't like the idea of spending the night waiting in vain for a ghost to show up, you might want to head out to Meridian Road in Rensselaer, where it is said that for decades, the ghost of Old Man Moody has been showing up for anyone who simply flashes their headlights.

The popular legend concerns a local farmer, Moody, and his son. One day, Moody's son was abducted from the family farm. As darkness fell, Moody took up a lantern and began searching the fields for his son. After several hours, Moody's lantern illuminated a horrifying sight; lying in the field was his son's lifeless, decapitated body. Overcome with grief, Moody decided he couldn't live without his son, so he put down his lantern and hanged himself from a tree near his son's body, not knowing that his actions would condemn his soul to wander the Earth for all eternity.

For decades, people have been driving out to the tree where Moody hanged himself, even though it's now just a stump. To summon the ghost, they flash their car headlights three times and then sit back and wait. Several minutes later, almost like clockwork, a small light (the color varies from red to orange to yellow) appears off in the distance and slowly moves forward. This light is said to be the ghost of Moody, carrying a lantern as he looks for his son or perhaps even his killer. After several minutes, the light simply blinks out or else vanishes in the field. Skeptics claim that the light is either a reflection off a street sign or else headlights from cars traveling on nearby roads. But those who have seen the light themselves have no doubt that it is Moody's ghost wandering the fields.

Central Indiana

MOST OF CENTRAL INDIANA IS PART OF THE TILL PLAINS, A RICH, FER-
tile area created by the elements left behind by the glaciers that
existed here so many years ago. It is this rich soil that accounts for
the wonderful crops farmers grow here year after year.

Central Indiana is also fertile ground for ghost stories. Many of
the popular ones incorporate elements from time-honored ghost
stories and relocate them to Indiana locales, leaving everyone who
hears them to wonder if the story is true or not. What's more, stories that originate in Central Indiana have a tendency to spread to
other areas of the state, where they grab a foothold and sprout new
variations as they go. Whether this is because of the fertile nature
of the region or perhaps a product of the vast network of highways
concentrated here, one thing is for sure: When it comes to ghost
stories, Central Indiana knows how to grow 'em!

The Little People Of The Mounds

Sitting in the shadow of the White River in Anderson is Mounds
State Park, which is composed of ten enigmatic structures that have
long perplexed the people who have witnessed them. Oh yeah, and
there's a bunch of creepy two-foot-tall robed creatures running
around in the woods here, too!

The mounds date back to around 150 B.C. As best as anyone can determine, they were created by the Adena culture, but were also used by the Hopewell. At the center of the smaller mounds is the aptly named Great Mound, which, at almost a quarter mile in diameter, is the largest structure of its kind in Indiana. There is also a wide, circular trench dug around the Great Mound that reaches more than ten feet in depth.

Part of the mystique surrounding these mounds is that it is still unclear what they were used for. Based on some excavations, it has been established that these mounds were not burial sites, leading to the popular theory that their purpose was ceremonial. But for what types of ceremonies?

Trying to determine that is like trying to find a needle in a haystack. That's because the mounds here were not treated very well. Over the years, various people came and poked, prodded, and dug up parts of the mounds. Some were looking for answers and others were looking for relics or other items of value. Either way, the result was that history was destroyed. The most damage to the mounds occurred in 1897, when the Indiana Union Traction Company bought up the land and built an amusement park among the mounds, complete with a carousel that was plopped right on top of the Great Mound.

The state of Indiana, however, soon stepped in to save the day. In 1930, after having the property donated to the state, officials put up protective fences and then reopened the area to the public as the new Mounds State Park. Today, visitors to the park can walk among tree-lined paths that wind their way down to and around the mounds. It is also along these paths that people have reported encountering dwarf-like robed creatures.

Those who have seen these creatures describe them as looking human in every way, save for one: they are only two feet tall. Wearing dark blue or purple robes, the creatures dart back and forth between the trees, watching visitors from a distance. Once spotted, the creatures jump up and run off into the woods. They are also seen moving along the shoreline of the White River nearby.

Now before you dismiss the reports of little creatures running around in the woods, consider this: The sightings date back hundreds of years. In fact, there is a local Delaware Indian legend that claims an entire tribe of the little beings live in the woods. The

Delaware referred to them as "Puk-wud-ies," which loosely translates to "little wild men of the forest."

Terror on Lovers' Lane

The term Lovers' Lane might not mean much to today's youth, but their parents almost certainly have memories of them—dark, secluded roads where enamored teens would go to park, listen to the radio, and make out. For teenagers in the 1950s and '60s, no matter where they lived in the United States, there was a local Lovers' Lane. The phenomenon was so large that cautionary urban legends developed to keep teens away from Lovers' Lanes.

It was not uncommon to hear tales of murder and mayhem associated with Lovers' Lanes. These stories were circulated by local teens to scare each other or by parents who were trying to keep their kids from parking and doing inappropriate things. Most stories involved a young couple going up to a Lovers' Lane to be alone, only to die a horrible death when attacked by a homicidal maniac wielding various weapons, from axes to giant hooks. The beauty of these tales was that they were filled with enough reality to make them appear to be true, while vague enough to make it nearly impossible to debunk them. Although some of these legends have faded into obscurity, the story associated with the Lovers' Lane off of Route 334 outside of Zionsville has survived all these years because it includes an interesting postscript to the tale—ghosts!

Back in the 1950s, Route 334 West was a totally different road. The houses dotting the roadside today didn't exist then. Instead, there was nothing but trees as far as the eye could see. It was along this stretch that a small, dead-end road became known as a Lovers' Lane. According to the legend, a young couple decided to sit here and get to know each other better.

Unbeknownst to the couple, there was a deranged madman lurking in the shadows, armed with an ax. It's doubtful the young couple knew of they were in danger until it was too late. When the deed was done, the killer placed both bodies under a tree at the dead end and disappeared, never to be heard from again.

For many years after the crime, people avoided Lovers' Lane, believing the killer was still out there awaiting more victims. Eventually, though, they began to slowly make their way out there again.

And that's when the ghost stories began. There were reports of disembodied screams—one male and one female—coming from near the tree where the bodies were discovered. Even today, while the Lovers' Lane itself is nearly forgotten, there are still reports of screams echoing through the remaining trees late at night.

Amy's Last Swim

Now known as the Shadyside Recreation Area, Aqua Gardens in Anderson has long been a wonderful place to visit, with scenic areas strategically placed around two lakes, perfect picnic spots, and several miles of walking trails through dozens of acres of natural beauty.

It was here in the 1960s that teenager Amy Chapman and a group of her friends decided to have an evening bonfire. For a while, the teenagers all sat around the roaring fire, telling stories, and just generally having a good time. As the night wore on, some of the group got bored and suggested they all take a late-night swim. Although Amy couldn't swim, she apparently didn't want to feel left out, and she agreed to go in the water with the others.

No one is sure what happened next. All of the kids who went swimming claimed they didn't hear or see anything strange or out of the ordinary. But when they all came back to shore, they noticed that Amy wasn't with them anymore. They had all seen her get in the water with everyone else, but not a single one of them saw her get out. A frantic search along the water's edge turned up nothing, so the teenagers rushed home to tell their parents that Amy was missing.

Sadly, Amy's body was found early the next morning, floating facedown in the water. After talking to the teenagers and reviewing the evidence, the police ruled Amy's death an unfortunate accident. It appeared that since Amy couldn't swim, she had simply drifted too far out into the water and drowned, all without her friends hearing a single sound.

As would be expected, after Amy's funeral, people avoided the area. It just brought up too many painful memories. But as time wore on, they returned. And that's when the ghost stories started.

People began seeing Amy's ghost, still soaking wet, at the water's edge, and she is still seen to this day. Sometimes her ghost just stands there, silently looking out over the water. At other times she is literally floating above the water. But on other occasions, her ghost appears to be trying to warn people, perhaps attempting to save them from the same watery grave that claimed her life.

Caution: Werewolf Crossing Ahead!

So you've been searching for ghosts for years now and you've become somewhat jaded. You're still into the paranormal, but you're looking for something a little bit different than the standard bump-in-the-night ghost story. Well, if that's the case, wait for the next full moon and take a road trip out to rural Shelbyville, Indiana. There, just off of East Union Road, you will find Short Blue Road. This is the road that will take you down into an area known locally as Werewolf Hollow—an area filled with all sorts of strange creatures and sights. And yes, even a werewolf.

The first warning sign you'll see as you prepare to enter Werewolf Hollow is an actual sign: a stop sign. This is no ordinary stop sign, however. Far from it. There are deep scratches in the sign. Whether the scratches were caused by man, beast, or something in between is still hotly debated. Either way, keep an eye on this sign as you pass by it. It is said to sometimes appear to be bleeding—yet another warning that you shouldn't press on.

But if you do go on, keep a sharp eye out for the apparition of a man standing alongside the road. He, too, is warning you not to go into the hollow, especially at night. Legend has it that if you drive past him, he will try to stop you by banging on your car and even trying to scratch his way inside.

As you reach the hollow, you will start to notice that the trees along each side of the road appear to come alive, stretching their branches out over the top of the road to create the surreal feeling that you are now driving in a tunnel. Eventually, you will see a small hill stretching out before you. It is said that near this spot, many years ago, a young boy wandered away from his family homestead under the light of a full moon. He was never seen or heard from again. Rumors soon spread through the area that the boy had been attacked and killed by a werewolf. Worse, the boy was now a werewolf himself and was roaming the countryside.

Legend has it that on nights with a full moon, if you stop your car while facing the hill, you will see the shadowy outline of a young boy walking along the roadside near the top of the hill. Suddenly, the boy's shadow will become distorted, as if some sort of transformation is taking place. Without warning, the mutated shape will dart across the top of the hill and disappear into the woods. At that point, don't be surprised if you start to hear howling and growling coming from all around your car. This is probably the best time to bid Werewolf Hollow farewell and leave posthaste.

Entombed in Concrete

In the early 1900s, as railroad lines were being run across the area outside of Avon, Indiana, workers ran into a quandary. How would they get the tracks across White Lick Creek and the road that is now CR 625? The solution was obvious: build a bridge. So around 1906, construction began on a massive concrete structure that would take the trains up and over the road and then the creek.

During construction, hundreds of workers were hired to help with the project. The most strenuous task was pouring concrete to fill in the huge pillars upon which the tracks would be placed. The wet concrete would be poured from wooden platforms that were stretched across the pillars.

One day, a worker standing on one of the platforms was preparing to pour the next batch of concrete into a partly filled pillar when he lost his balance. For a split second, it looked like he might be able to right himself. But then, he fell, dropping straight down into the pillar. The worker screamed out for help as he tried to stay afloat in the quicksandlike wet cement. His coworkers rushed to his aid but were unable to reach him, as he was down too far in the pillar. They could only stand by and watch helplessly as the man was slowly pulled down deeper and deeper. Finally, the man gave out one last choked scream and then disappeared below the surface of the concrete.

Badly shaken, the site managers had to make a decision regarding the man's body. They felt they should exhume it, but to do that would mean breaking the pillar and wasting tons of concrete. Plus, they had a deadline to meet and all the additional work would certainly put them way behind schedule. So the decision was made to leave the man's body where it was and carry on with the construction. The rest of the workers agreed, but the decision did not sit well with them. Some say that the decision didn't go over too well with the dead man, either, and that if you're at the bridge at just the right time, you can hear his objections for yourself.

For years now, people have heard all sorts of strange sounds coming from the concrete bridge. There are banging noises that sound like they are coming from inside the pillars, as if someone is trying desperately to get out. Most unsettling of all, however, are the disembodied screams that often echo through the area.

The Blue Lady

In the Roaring Twenties, Pendleton Pike through McCordsville was a hotbed of activity, with everyone from locals to gangsters traveling up and down it. So when the Plantation Club was erected at the corner of West Pendleton Pike and Carroll Road, it soon became the place to be. Before long, gangsters moved in, attracting all sorts of shady dealings, from illegal gambling and alcohol smuggling to prostitution. It is even said that John Dillinger himself would stop in from time to time to unwind when he was "between jobs."

Despite—or maybe because of—all the illegal activity, the Plantation Club thrived and soon began to expand. The property grew to include almost fifty acres. Several small cabins were erected around a lake on the property so that the ladies of the evening who worked the club could entertain their clients away from the prying eyes of the general public. It was at one of these cabins where the legend of the Blue Lady was born.

According to the legend, one of the prostitutes who worked there was entertaining a client inside one of the cabins when something went wrong. Dreadfully wrong. Exactly what happened is unknown, but when it was over, the young woman was dead. Word quickly spread among the other prostitutes that if they knew what was good for them, they would keep their mouths shut about the murder and just go back to business as usual. The murdered girl, or rather her ghost, had other ideas. Almost immediately after the woman's death, her ghost began making appearances in and around the cabin. Stranger still, her ghost always appeared to be bathed in a weird, blue mist. Not wanting to get in any trouble, the other working girls quietly began avoiding the cabin and would only speak in hushed tones among themselves about the Blue Lady.

Once alcohol became legal again and the FBI started cracking down on gangsters, fewer people started showing up at the Plantation Club. Eventually, it fell into disrepair and was abandoned. In the 1960s, Chuck Nickerson saw opportunity in the property and purchased it, turning it into an events facility that could hold up to thirty-five thousand people. Nickerson even had rides installed throughout the property and built a pavilion alongside the lake near the infamous Blue Lady cabin. Apparently, the Blue Lady approved of the pavilion, because her ghost started showing up there, much to the chagrin, or in some cases excitement, of guests.

In January 1988, Doni and Michael Nickerson purchased the entire property with the intent of restoring it to the way it was during the days of the Plantation Club. After several major renovations, the property was once again open to the public, this time under the name Casino's.

It would appear that restoring the property to the style of the Roaring Twenties made the ghosts from that era feel right at home. That's because, shortly after it reopened, strange things began happening inside Casino's. Doors opened and closed on their own, glasses and other objects moved without being touched, and footsteps echoed through the building when no one else was around. As for the Blue Lady, she continued to be sighted on a regular basis, although she preferred to hang out near the lake as opposed to coming inside the building.

Casino's, too, would eventually close and several years ago, all of the buildings, including the Blue Lady cabin, were knocked down to make way for a golf driving range. Even that facility was short lived, and today, nothing remains at the site except a huge vacant lot, a small lake . . . and a ghost. Even though all the structures are gone, from time to time, a ghostly woman surrounded by a weird blue mist is seen standing near the edge of the lake.

Screams at Midnight and a Bloody Yellow Dress

I have been studying ghosts and folklore for more than twenty-six years. During that time, I have yet to come across a college campus without stories of hauntings. In fact, it's rare to come across a non-haunted building anywhere on university property. It's as if students, having moved out of their family homes for the first time, feel the need to bring all their hometown ghost stories with them and attach them to random campus buildings and locations. Couple that with large groups of young adults living away from familiar surroundings and you have fertile ground for ghost stories to thrive. Indiana University is no different. It is said to be practically crawling with ghosts. But one campus building, Read Hall, stands above the rest. Here, there are two ghosts battling it out to see which one ranks as the hall's number one spooky specter.

The first ghost is the result of a violent and deadly disagreement between a young girl with long black hair and her boyfriend, a pre-med student who lived on the third floor of Read Hall. The fateful evening began innocently enough, with the couple going out for a night on the town. At the end of the evening, the girl, wearing a stunning yellow dress, accompanied her boyfriend up to his dorm room on the third floor. Apparently, the couple got into a disagreement, which quickly escalated. The argument got more and more heated, until the boy, in a fit of rage, reached into his medical bag, grabbed a scalpel, and slashed the young girl to death. When the heinous act was done, the boy attempted to cover it up by hiding the body in the tunnels in Read Hall's basement. The girl's body, still in the blood-stained yellow dress, was discovered and the boy was quickly arrested.

What became of the boy is unclear; versions of the tale have him going to prison or a mental institution and even hanging himself. As for the girl, while her body was buried, her spirit is said to appear at Read Hall. Late at night, students have seen the disturbing image of a young girl in a blood-stained yellow dress gliding down the hallway.

The second spirit at Read Hall is also a woman, but she prefers to hang out on the sixth floor. Unlike the girl in the yellow dress, this ghost has a name, Paula. As the story goes, Paula was a resident assistant at Read Hall. The December before Paula was to graduate, she began to hear rumors that her grades might not be high enough for her to graduate. Unable to convince herself otherwise, Paula began to look upon herself as a failure. On the night of December 12, as the time was drawing close to midnight, Paula made the harsh decision to take her own life. She climbed the staircase up to the sixth floor and then threw herself down the stairwell, breaking her neck.

It is said that every December 12 around midnight, the bone-chilling scream of a young girl can be heard, as Paula's last moments are played out on the stairwell.

The Ghostly Children of Heady Hollow

I don't know about you, but of all the different types of ghosts out there, the ones that creep me out the most are those of children. Maybe it's the whole idea that children are supposed to represent innocence, not sadness and eternal unrest. Or maybe I was scarred at an early age by too many late-night viewings of Stanley Kubrick's *The Shining*. Either way, I made sure that when I was putting this book together, I didn't linger too long in the area in Fishers known as Heady Hollow. That's because it's supposed to be haunted not by just one ghostly child, but a whole slew of them!

Heady Hollow, named after the Heady family who once lived in the area, lies near the intersection of Allisonville Road and East 126th Street. Today, it's a wooded area, but as the story goes, back in the 1800s, the Heady family ran a schoolhouse here. One day, a fire broke out in the school, destroying the entire building. Several children were also killed in the blaze. After their funerals, their tiny bodies were all laid to rest in Heady Cemetery, which sits roughly a mile from the hollow.

Today, it is said that on certain nights, the ghosts of the children killed in the fire rise up from their graves and gather at the main entrance to the cemetery. They stand silent for a while, as if they are waiting to ensure all are present and accounted for. Then they walk, en masse, down the street to Heady Hollow, the scene of their demise. Once they arrive at the hollow, they again stand silent and then simply vanish.

Historians are quick to point out that while there was indeed a Heady family who lived in the area, there are no records indicating that a school ever stood in Heady Hollow. Apparently that has not stopped the ghosts from congregating there.

Summoning the Blue Lady

The Story Inn is all that remains of the village of Story. Dr. George Story came to the area and received a land grant in 1851. The village sprang up almost overnight, and the general store was one of the very first buildings erected.

At its height, Story was a thriving village, complete with its own schoolhouse and post office. All that changed during the Great Depression, though, when people began leaving the area in droves. When the United States Army Corps of Engineers flooded the area in 1960 to create Lake Monroe, Story was essentially cut off from most neighboring towns. Little by little, the people moved on, leaving nothing but the general store behind.

In the early 1980s, Cynthia Schultz and her handyman friend, Benjamin (whose last name has been lost), purchased the general store and turned it into a restaurant and B&B called the Story Inn. The main floor served as the restaurant and the second floor held several guest rooms. One of these rooms is called the Blue Lady Room, after the ghost said to haunt it.

It wasn't always named the Blue Lady Room, though. At the inn, blank journals had been placed inside each room for guests to write about their experiences. Most of the journals from the other rooms are filled with descriptions of romantic weekends and fun-filled family getaways. The journal from this room, however, contains bizarre entries detailing encounters with a ghostly woman. One entry referred to her as the Blue Lady, and the name apparently caught on, because as new guests wrote of their experiences, they, too, referred to her as the "Blue Lady." And so, in 2001, the decision was made to officially change the name of the room to the Blue Lady Room.

The interesting thing about the Blue Lady ghost is that she does not wear blue. Instead, she is seen wearing a long white dress or robe. The name comes from the blue lamp on the nightstand that summons the lady when guests turn it on. She doesn't appear immediately, though. And in some cases, guests have drifted off to sleep before seeing her, only to awake suddenly in the middle of the night to the sight of the Blue Lady standing alongside their bed.

So far, no one has recognized the identity of the ghost. Dr. Story had been married several times, so it is believed to be one of his former wives. Or maybe she was just a former resident or guest who fell in love with the place and decided to stick around for a while. Either way, if you're looking for a good meal and a unique place to spend the night, check in to the Story Inn and be sure to ask for the Blue Lady Room.

Azalia's Crybaby Bridge

One of the most fascinating themes in modern ghost stories is something known as a "crybaby bridge." The basic story involves a bridge, a new mother, and her infant child. The main storyline is usually a tragic occurrence on the bridge, typically resulting in the baby's death. The tale ends with people going to the bridge and hearing the baby's cries. Crybaby bridge stories exist throughout the United States, with the overwhelming number of them being centered in the Midwest. As far as Indiana is concerned, the most popular crybaby bridge is located just outside the tiny town of Azalia.

The story takes place in the late 1800s, when one young girl living in Azalia discovered she was pregnant. In that time, having a child out of wedlock would surely bring shame to the girl and her entire family, but she could not bring herself to terminate the pregnancy. She therefore resigned herself to having the child. There was no way, however, that she could have prepared herself for when her parents disowned her after the child was born.

The young girl tried hard to raise the child alone, but she found it nearly impossible, and with no one to turn to, she one day just snapped. After sitting silently with her child the entire day, upon nightfall, the young woman wrapped her child in a blanket and headed out towards the bridge located on the southwest outskirts of town.

Upon reaching the bridge, the woman stood there with the baby in her arms. Then, she did something unspeakable: she threw her baby off the bridge into the water below. Then she simply walked back home.

The next day, people noticed the young woman, now dressed all in black, walking all alone out to the bridge on the edge of town. And while they may have wondered where her baby was, it was none of their business, so they kept their questions to themselves. As the weeks and then months rolled by, the townsfolk got used to the familiar sight of the young woman standing alongside the bridge, always dressed in black, simply staring down at the water. Then one day, the woman was gone, never to be seen again.

There are those who believe the young woman and her baby never left that bridge. As proof, they say that if you go to the bridge on nights with a full moon, you will see the ghost of a young woman dressed in black, standing on the side and staring down into the water. And that if you listen carefully, you just might be able to make out the muffled cries of an infant child coming from somewhere under the bridge.

The Ghosts of Stepp Cemetery

I'm not sure why, but most of Indiana's creepiest locations tend to be inside state forests. If you're looking for something really scary, you might want to head over to the Morgan-Monroe State Forest, located near Martinsville, where you'll be able to step inside what many consider to be one of the most haunted locations in the entire United States—Stepp Cemetery.

The ghost stories and legends associated with Stepp Cemetery have been around for years. In fact, you'd be hard-pressed to find any Hoosier under the age of sixty who hasn't heard of Stepp. Little is known about the origins of the cemetery other than it was established sometime in the early 1800s. But even that is a bit fuzzy, especially when you hear some people claim it was the work of a mysterious cult known as the Crabbites.

While most of the gravestones are from the first half of the 1800s, there are a few from the late 1700s. There are even a few family plots here, such as the Bowmans and the Adkins. Unfortunately, Stepp Cemetery has fallen victim to repeated vandalism over the years, making it hard to get a firm count on how many people are at rest here.

One of the most enduring stories concerns the Witch's Throne, an old tree stump that resembles a throne. It is said that a woman dressed entirely in black sits here, often under the light of a full moon. Sometimes she is even seen holding her face in her hands and weeping, her painful sobs often being heard even before one reaches the cemetery. There is a story concerning a call to a local police station claiming a woman was up in Stepp Cemetery crying. Police arrived and heard the crying, too. But when they reached the cemetery, the crying suddenly stopped and the cemetery was found to be empty.

Who the Woman in Black weeps for is unknown. Some say it is one of her children who is buried in the cemetery. In another variation her child is not buried here, but instead was murdered inside the cemetery and her body left behind. In this version, the ghostly woman is weeping over the loss of her child as she sits and waits to see if the murderer returns to the scene of the crime. Yet another variation says that the woman is crying over the loss of her husband, a local construction worker, who was killed while working and later buried at Stepp.

Another ghost said to haunt Stepp Cemetery is known as Baby Lester, the name deriving from a headstone in Stepp marked simply "Baby Lester 1937." Originally, it was thought that the Woman in Black was Baby Lester's mother, which turned out to not be true when Lester's mother, Olethia Walls, was found to be very much alive (she passed away in 2001). But that did not stop people from hearing the cries of a baby in the cemetery late at night. It is also not uncommon to find Baby Lester's grave covered with coins and other small trinkets that have been left behind by cemetery visitors as a tribute.

One final ghost story, and a late addition to the game, says that there are a couple of giant black dogs that roam the cemetery grounds at night, protecting it from all who might enter to try and vandalize this sacred ground. The dogs are said to walk around the perimeter of the cemetery, sticking mainly to the woods. They seem to be able to sense when people are there to cause harm and will come charging into the cemetery with their eyes sometimes glowing a fiery red.

Indianapolis

MANY PEOPLE ARE UNAWARE THAT INDIANAPOLIS WASN'T THE FIRST choice to be the capital of Indiana. In fact, when Indianapolis became the capital in 1825, two other cities had already been the capital: Vincennes was the territorial capital in 1809, and in 1813, the government moved to Corydon. Today, not only is Indianapolis the largest city in the state, but it's also the second-largest of all U.S. capitals. It seems everything associated with this city echoes the motto, "go big or go home." Even the Indianapolis Motor Speedway is recognized as the sporting venue with the largest seating capacity in the world at 857,000 seats. So when it comes to ghosts in Indianapolis, why wouldn't you expect them to adhere to that same motto?

No, I'm not going to tell you that there are giant forty-foot ghosts roaming downtown Indianapolis. The ghosts of Indianapolis, however, do tend to be found in big mansions and buildings in the city. So if you find yourself ghosthunting in Indianapolis, here's a bit of advice: Start with the biggest building you can find. As some of the following stories will attest, you just might get lucky and see a ghost.

Riverdale's Haunted Pool

James Ashbury Allison was born on August 11, 1872, in Macellus, Michigan. He moved with his family to Indiana at the age of two and eventually arrived in Indianapolis in 1880. From an early age, Allison adopted the belief that if he needed something and it wasn't readily available, he would just create his own. A prime example of this was when he grew frustrated by the less-than-satisfactory pens he was using for writing. This led him to create his own Allison Perfection Fountain Pen.

In the early 1900s, Allison began working on a series of business ventures that would make him a very rich man. Most notably, in 1910, he cofounded the Indianapolis Motor Speedway. It was also around this time that Allison and his wife, Sarah, whom he had married in 1907, began the initial plans for what would become their dream mansion.

In 1910, Allison and his wife bought more than sixty acres on Cold Springs Road. The actual construction began the following year in 1911. Things got off to a good start, but Allison's desire to spare no expense and create the greatest mansion in Indianapolis soon brought construction to a screeching halt. After visiting his neighbors' mansions, he would return home and change his plans. He eventually fired the original architect and replaced him with the one who had designed the home of his friend and neighbor, Frank Wheeler.

During the construction, Allison wanted to ensure that his mansion was built with the finest materials available. It is said that an entire species of trees became extinct because he used it all up for the mansion. He even flew in artists from Europe to add their unique flair for design to the home.

Allison's attention to detail extended from his house to the grounds and gardens; he hired world-famous landscaper and architect Jens Jensen, and the final version of the plans for the grounds included an orchard, a rose garden, several spring-fed ponds, and even two marble staircases.

The mansion, named Riverdale, was completed in 1914 with a final price tag hovering somewhere around $2 million. In addition to all of the usual accouterments one would expect to find in a sprawling mansion, Riverdale also included a marble aviary filled with exotic birds, a music room containing a two-story pipe organ, an indoor pool in the basement, and even a central vacuum system.

James and Sarah lived in Riverdale until 1928, when they divorced and Sarah moved out. The following month, James remarried, but he passed away a few months later at the age of fifty-six. Upon his death, Allison's mother, Myra, inherited Riverdale and lived there until she passed away. The mansion was eventually purchased by the Sisters of St. Francis, who in 1937 made it part of Marian College, where it remains today.

There have been reports of hauntings at Riverdale, although no ghosts have ever been seen here. Instead, objects move from room to room as if someone or something is rearranging things. Some of the furniture has been known to move on its own, too. The room with the most activity is the library, where entire groups of books are said to move from shelf to shelf. Most people believe all this moving is being done by the ghost of James Allison himself.

The setting for the best-known ghost story attached to the mansion is the indoor pool in the basement. According to legend, a baby was left unattended near the pool only for an instant. But that was all it took for the baby to fall into the pool and drown. There are reports of the sounds of a baby crying in the pool area, even when there's no one present.

Ghosts in the Old Bordello

It is the oldest commercial building in Indianapolis and the oldest continually operating bar in the state. It could also hold claim to an award for the bar with the strangest name. Based on the number of reported ghost sightings inside the building, a case could be made that the Slippery Noodle Inn is one of downtown Indianapolis's most haunted buildings.

The establishment was known as the Tremont House when its doors opened for the first time in 1850. Although the bar on the main floor has always remained the center of attention, even during Prohibition, it seems that the most supernatural activity has taken place on the top floor and in the basement.

In the nineteenth century, the property was used as a stop on the Underground Railroad, with numerous fugitive slaves being hidden away here as they made their attempt to flee bondage in the

South. Obviously, no records from this time mention how many slaves passed through the building or even how they were kept hidden away while they were here. But the common belief is that once a slave arrived, he or she was secreted away to the basement and kept there until the coast was clear and they could be moved to another building and closer to freedom.

During Prohibition, beer was made illegally in the basement and served in the upstairs bar when it was safe to do so. Of course, this attracted the attention of outlaws and soon the establishment was filled with many shady characters. Legend has it that even infamous gangster John Dillinger liked to hang out here, with more than a few people believing he is responsible for the bullet holes in the old horse stable behind the main building.

One good vice deserves another, so it was around this time that a bordello was opened up above the main floor. Composed of a short hallway with rooms on either side, this new addition allowed the ladies of the evening to offer their services to the men at the bar and then bring any interested parties upstairs for a little alone time. The bordello is said to have remained open until sometime around 1953, when legend states that two men got into a quarrel over one of the working women. The fight turned violent, with one man stabbing the other to death and leaving the bloody knife on the bar as he fled out into the street.

In 1963, the building was purchased by Harold and Lorean Yeagy, who gave it the name Slippery Noodle Inn. As for the meaning behind the name, it apparently was just something random that happened to sound good. Today, the building is looked after by the Yeagys' son.

Bring up the subject of ghosts at the Slippery Noodle Inn and you'll find that while the occasional glass might move and a light or two might flicker downstairs, the bulk of the ghostly activity is said to take place upstairs in the rooms once used by the ladies of the bordello. It would appear that at least one of the ladies who worked here has decided to hang around.

The doors to the rooms open and close on their own. On more than one occasion, a Noodle employee has stood at the top of the stairs, looking down the hallway, only to see the doors to the rooms open and close one by one as if something was walking down the hall and hitting each individual door. The ghost also apparently doesn't like when men come into its domain. Males standing in the upstairs hallway have reported being pushed, hit, and even slapped in the face.

Skiles Test and His House of Blue Lights

When he was alive, millionaire Skiles Test was many different things to many different people—a successful businessman, an eccentric, an inventor, an architect—but he will be forever remembered for living in a building that is one of the strangest and most haunted places in Indiana, the House of Blue Lights.

Born in 1889, Test had an insatiable appetite for learning new things. He wanted to know about anything and everything. And although he was an heir to the enormous Diamond Chain Company fortune, he wanted to make a name for himself, too. So as he grew older, Test got involved in several business ventures, all of which were successful, most notably his serving as president of Indianapolis Motor Inns and his own company, Test Realty Corporation. All this meant that Test was a millionaire by the time he reached his early twenties.

In 1913, Test married Josephine Denges. At around the same time, he began buying up land around Indianapolis, including approximately eighty acres and a small farmhouse along what is today known as Fall Creek Road. This is the spot where Test built his dream home, but more than that, the ample acreage, as well as what appeared to be money to burn, allowed Test to fuel his yearning to create anything his heart desired.

Test first set his mind to renovating the farmhouse. The most stunning additions were entire walls made of glass block. Over the years, Test built an amazing and mind-boggling series of structures on his property, and he installed a miniature railroad that allowed him to travel across his immense tract of land. Knowing that winter weather would make it impossible for the railroad to run, Test built a series of tunnels that allowed him to move from building to building. But by all accounts, Test saved his best work for his swimming pool.

Using a massive forty-by-eighty-foot pool as his starting point, Test decided he wanted to have several diving boards, all at varying heights. As far as he was concerned, having a simple ladder to get to the diving boards was the easy way out, so he built a multistory bathhouse, complete with a basement, with the diving boards emerging from the structure. Test even installed an elevator to shuttle divers from floor to floor.

But why a basement? Well, not only could Test use it to house all of the machinery for the pool, but because he had used glass block along the bottom of the pool, he could string colored lights below them, thereby illuminating the water at night. Test even developed a motorized surfboard for the pool!

If there was one thing that Test loved more than inventing things, it was animals. While the property was at first home to just a few dogs and barn cats, the number of animals soon grew to well over two hundred. Rumor has it that there were so many animals that Test employed staff members whose sole responsibility was to feed and look after them all. That job, of course, also required employees to take on a very odd task. Whenever an animal passed away on the property, Test would have the employee place it in a casket and give it a formal burial in the pet cemetery located on the property, complete with its own little limestone tombstone with copper nameplate. It is said that at one point, just to make sure they were ready for any unexpected deaths, staff members had built up a stockpile of tiny tombstones and coffins.

Needless to say, with all of these unique and exciting things to see on the Test property, many people wanted to visit. So it's no surprise that the house became the site of many lavish parties, which Test and Josephine enjoyed to no end. They would decorate the entire property, especially during the Christmas season, when Test wove endless strings of blue lights—blue was his favorite color—through the trees.

But things were not all fun and games in the Test household, and as the years rolled on, Skiles and Josephine grew further and further apart. One Christmas in the 1930s, the blue lights went up and never came back down. Shortly thereafter, the couple divorced and Josephine moved off the property. And with that, all the components were finally in place for the birth of the House of Blue Lights.

No one is really sure when the legend originated, but once it started, it spread like wildfire across Indianapolis. According to the legend, Josephine had passed away, which sent Skiles into a deep

depression. Unable to part with her, Skiles decided to instead keep her body at the farmhouse, entombed inside a glass casket. He often resorted to spending entire evenings sitting silently by Josephine's casket, overcome with grief. Further, it was alleged that the blue lights were Test's tribute to his departed wife, as blue was said to be her favorite color.

In truth, Josephine was still alive and well: in fact, she would outlive Skiles by almost fifteen years. Still, local teenagers and curiosity seekers would sneak on the property under cover of darkness in an attempt to see the dead Mrs. Test lying in a glass casket. This gave rise to another rumor—that Test had trained a group of attack dogs to stand guard over the casket and chase away trespassers. Even so, dozens of people still claimed to have caught a glimpse of Skiles Test sitting quietly beside a glass casket, bathed in blue light.

But just what were these people seeing? Were they simply mistaking one of the tiny caskets made for the farmhouse pets as the one that housed Josephine? Possibly, but the caskets for the pets were made of wood, not glass. And as stated earlier, Josephine was still alive. So what or who was lying in the casket?

That was the question all of Indianapolis was asking when Skiles Test passed away on March 19, 1964. And they got their chance to find out when it was announced that a public auction was going to be held on the property to sell off Test's material goods. When auctioneers arrived on the property to assess the situation, they were so overwhelmed with the amount of things that they decided they would need to hold a three-day auction if they were to ever stand a chance of getting rid of everything.

During that auction, it is estimated that more than fifty thousand people crammed onto the property. And while most were looking to just find a bargain, there's no denying that everyone was keeping their eyes peeled for a glass casket that might be holding human remains. And while there were huge stockpiles of foodstuffs, household items, and tiny wooden caskets, not a single glass casket was found. As for the blue lights, they were sold off to a buyer whose name remains a mystery.

Test's will called for the property, including the farmhouse and all outbuildings, to be turned over to the Department of Parks and Recreation and made into a Boy Scout camp. After many years of legal wrangling, the decision was made to abandon plans for the camp and instead turn it into a nature park. In 1978, the Test farmhouse and all the outbuildings, including the pool house, were demolished. But even the destruction of the house itself wasn't enough to keep the House of Blue Lights legend down.

Although nothing remains of the house, visitors to the Skiles Test Nature Park have reported encountering something unexplained along its many trails. In the evening hours, the woods near where the Test farmhouse once stood are said to come alive with mysterious blue lights, which move throughout the trees as if they have minds of their own. There is also supposed to be one spot in particular where it appears as if the entire area is bathed in an eerie blue glow.

The Smell of Death at Hannah House

When Alexander Hannah began funding the construction of his Madison Avenue dream home on the south side of Indianapolis, he was just looking for a place to live. It ended up serving a much bigger purpose, part of which might have led to the hauntings of the home that continue to this day.

Completed in 1858, the house soon became a stop on the Underground Railroad, harboring escaped slaves on their way to Canada. The secretive nature of the organization meant few records were kept, so there is no way of telling just how many refugees Hannah helped or where they were hidden. It is believed, however, that most were hidden away in the basement.

One night in the basement, according to one story, one of the escaped slaves accidentally knocked over a lantern. Soon, a large part of the basement was on fire, and as the flames spread, some of the refugees began to burn. Hannah and the other slaves managed to contain the fire before it spread to the rest of the house, but they were unable to save the lives of the burn victims. Legend has it that the victims were secretly buried in the basement of the house.

Hannah, a prominent figure in Indiana history, originally built the house for himself his staff, but at age fifty-one, he married Elizabeth Jackson, and another wing was added on for the servants.

Hannah and Elizabeth remained in Hannah House until the late 1890s, at which point it was sold off. There is no evidence that the Hannahs experienced anything paranormal inside the house. The next owners, however, quickly became convinced that there was something weird going on in the basement. Not knowing that escaped slaves were allegedly buried down there, the new family dismissed the strange noises as normal sounds that old houses make. The one thing they couldn't ignore was the overpowering odor of what could only be described as "death" that would waft through the house.

Eventually, word leaked out about the bodies that might be in the basement. Suddenly, it all came together and made sense. Interestingly enough, once people began talking openly about what happened in the basement, the smell of death began to dissipate and then went away altogether. Of course, there was still the occasional odd noise or groaning that emanated from the basement, but overall, things calmed down considerably. Maybe that's why the Hannahs decided to move back in. Their ghosts, that is!

In the upstairs rooms, doors and windows began to open and close on their own. Chandeliers moved by themselves, too. There was also what sounded like people talking in hushed tones. An older woman, believed to be Elizabeth Hannah, is also seen walking around on the top floors. As for Alexander Hannah, his ghost has been seen throughout the building, although he seems to prefer hanging out near the balcony area.

The Ghostly Carriage Ride at Hawkeye

In the early 1900s, if you were a mover and a shaker in Indianapolis, you built a mansion along Cold Spring Road, known to the locals as Millionaires' Row. So that's exactly what successful businessman Frank Wheeler did. Like the others who had built their dream homes here, Wheeler wanted to make sure his really stuck out. So he hired Philadelphia architect William Price to create a mansion like no other. Price worked the next three years, from 1911 until 1914, to finish Hawkeye, the name Wheeler gave to the mansion. The result of all that hard work was nothing short of jaw-dropping.

The main house stood two stories tall and was made of brick, with green Spanish tile on the roof. Everywhere inside the mansion were examples of stunning craftsmanship—hand-carved staircase bannisters, imported tiles laid in intricate patterns, and sparkling chandeliers.

An impressive addition to the outside of the mansion was a porte cochere, a covered structure that allowed carriages to pull up to an entrance to drop off passengers without exposing them to any inclement weather. Originally designed in the late eighteenth century in Europe for castles and churches, the feature gained popularity among the wealthy in the United States in the early 1900s.

The grounds around the mansion were equally as stunning. Sitting in the middle of a custom-designed Japanese garden was a teahouse. Across the grounds was a large reflecting pool and a massive six-story observation tower from which one could survey the entire property in all its splendor. Perhaps James Allison, Wheeler's friend who was also building his own mansion nearby, went up into this tower to get a bird's-eye view of Price's handiwork. If he did, that might have been what prompted Allison to go home, fire his current architect, and hire Price to complete the work on the Allison mansion.

Life at Hawkeye was originally quite happy for Wheeler and his family. He always enjoyed entertaining people, and as a result, there was hardly a weekend when Hawkeye wasn't filled with laughter and music. Even the teahouse in the Japanese garden was hopping on weekends. But as Wheeler grew older, he started developing health problems, including what some believe may have been depression. It all ended one day when Wheeler walked into one of Hawkeye's many bathrooms and promptly shot himself in the head with a double-barreled shotgun. He was fifty-seven.

With the death of Frank Wheeler, the mansion was sold to the William Stokely family, who lived there until it was acquired by Marian College in 1960. The college still owns the building and currently uses it to house their admissions department.

Ghostly activity is reported at Hawkeye. Although it would make sense that Wheeler is haunting the building, considering the tragic way he ended his life, no one is really sure who the ghosts are. But they're clearly not Wheeler.

There are typical reports of odd noises and cold spots, but every once in a while, a mysterious scene plays out at Hawkeye's porte cochere, complete with props.

It has been said that from time to time, a ghostly carriage appears out of nowhere and stops at the porte cochere. Several seconds later, the ghost of a woman with brunette hair comes out of Hawkeye and gets into the carriage. The carriage then pulls away from the porte cochere and promptly vanishes.

Elias Jacoby Never Really Left Us

Up until the 1880s, there was no official Shriner organization in Indianapolis. That changed on June 4, 1884, when the Indianapolis Shriners were given a charter. The group quickly drew interest, and within a year, they had grown to more than one hundred members.

In the early 1900s, the decision was made that the Shriners in Indianapolis needed an official temple for meetings, so in 1909, the Murat Temple was built. Construction and additions continued for the next few years, resulting in an enormous building that houses two stages, one in a concert hall capable of seating eighteen hundred people and the other in a twenty-five-hundred-seat theater. There are also many rooms and halls for hosting events, the largest being the Egyptian Room, which can hold up to two thousand people. To date, the building remains the largest Shrine temple in the entire United States.

By all accounts, the resident ghost here is Elias J. Jacoby, a Shriner who was also the potentate when the temple was being built. He served as Imperial Potentate for all of North America from 1918 until 1919. Jacoby is said to have so loved the temple that he wished to spend every waking minute inside the glorious building. In fact, Jacoby passed away on December 31, 1935 while preparing for a New Year's Eve party at the temple. It only makes sense that Jacoby's ghost would return to the place that he loved so much while he was alive.

Jacoby's ghost seems to prefer hanging out in the temple's theater, just as Jacoby had done while he was alive. The first ghostly activity in the theater that has been attributed to his spirit occured when someone standing on stage noticed that one of the seats seemed to have an odd blue glow about it. As the man watched, the blue light rose up out of the seat and came towards the stage. It hovered near the stage for a few moments and then disappeared. When the man walked over to the seat, he was shocked to see that it was not only situated in Elias Jacoby's personal box, but it was the very seat Jacoby liked to claim for his own.

On another occasion, a temple employee was working in the theater when he caught something moving out of the corner of his eye. Looking up towards the balcony, he saw the ghostly image of a man sitting in one of the rocking chairs. Not believing his own eyes, the employee left the theater and went out into the hallway that contains the Shrine Club. As the employee's eyes wandered across the various paintings, they came to rest on one in particular—the portrait of Elias Jacoby. When the employee realized that the ghost he had just seen was the spitting image of Jacoby, he quit on the spot.

Jacoby's ghost apparently has taken a liking to the portrait. Employees on numerous occasions have seen a man dressed in a blue cloak walking down the hallway and then promptly disappearing into the painting.

As if more proof was needed, several psychics were brought into the temple in the 1990s to try and confirm once and for all if the building is haunted and, if so, by whom. To a person, they all confirmed that Jacoby was indeed the spirit haunting the temple. They also said that although Jacoby's spirit often moves about the temple, he prefers to stay inside the theater.

It is a common belief that doing any sort of renovations on a building will awaken spirits, as if the ghosts are curious what these strangers are doing to their former homes and places of business. This might be the case with the temple and Jacoby's ghost. In the late 1990s, when major renovations began in the temple, the number of reported sightings of Jacoby's ghost skyrocketed. His ghost is most active during renovations. The most mind-boggling report came one night when several people, including the Murat's public relations director, Lloyd Walton, watched as Jacoby's portrait began to morph, eventually appearing as if it were crying. Some took this as a sign that Jacoby was unhappy with the renovations. Others, though, thought Jacoby might have been upset over what had become of his portrait. You see, when everyone witnessed it crying, the portrait was laying in the attic, where it had been placed during the renovations. Whatever the case may be, renovations were recently completed and the number of ghost sightings has dropped considerably. Of course, Jacoby's portrait has since been returned to its rightful place on the wall in the building's Shrine Club.

Tragedy at the Coliseum

When it opened on the Indiana State Fairgrounds in the fall of 1939, the Coliseum was easily the largest event facility of its kind. With over eleven thousand seats, it quickly became the venue of choice for traveling shows, concerts, and sporting events. John F. Kennedy even spoke here in 1960 as part of his presidential campaign.

On Halloween night in 1963, more than four thousand people showed up at the Coliseum to enjoy the Holiday on Ice show. Unknown to everyone in attendance, as well as Coliseum employees, there was a faulty valve on one of the propane tanks used to help heat prepopped popcorn. As the show progressed, no one could know that propane gas was building up inside the enclosed Coliseum. At approximately 11:04, things reached their breaking point and an explosion rocked the Coliseum, sending bodies more than fifty feet into the air. Minutes later, a second blast ripped through the building, causing huge portions of concrete to come crashing down on the audience.

When the initial dust settled, those who weren't injured quickly started digging through the debris in an attempt to find other survivors. In some instances, they were only guided by the moans and cries of the injured. Sadly, sixty-five people died almost instantly from the explosion. Another nine eventually succumbed to their injuries. More than four hundred men, women, and children were injured by the blast, making it one of the worst disasters in Indiana history.

When all of the injured had been moved to local hospitals, a call was made to coroner Dennis Nicholas to come out and help with the processing of all the deceased. Upon arriving at the Coliseum, Nicholas realized he had a problem on his hands. Namely, with so many bodies to identify, where would he find a location big enough to house them all? Nicholas came up with the unique decision to turn the floor of the Coliseum into a huge, makeshift morgue. So, after all of the deceased were arranged on blankets and cots on the floor of the Coliseum, friends and family members were allowed to walk up and down the rows, viewing the remains. Those in attendances said it was one of the most somber and depressing scenes they have ever witnessed.

Today, even though many years have passed and the building is now known as the Pepsi Coliseum, there still seems to be some sort of residual ghostly energy from the night of the explosion lingering inside. Reports claiming that those sitting in Section 13, said to have been at the center of the explosion, have often been overcome with a sense of sadness and of not being alone.

Additionally, several members of the Coliseum staff, speaking on the condition of anonymity, said they have felt ghostly presences on the portions of the Coliseum floor that may have been used for the makeshift morgue.

Southern Indiana

IF YOU'VE EVER VISITED CERTAIN PARTS OF THE SOUTHERN UNITED STATES, you've probably noticed that once you get away from the hustle and bustle of the main cities, time tends to move a little slower. People just seem to take their time going about their business. And the old-timers will tell you about how good things were "way back when." Southern Indiana is no different. And not only do the people of Southern Indiana believe in the power of tradition, but even their ghost stories harken back to simpler times.

You can tell a Southern Indiana ghost story almost right from the start. This is because the settings tend to be older, more traditional buildings as opposed to modern facilities. There are no haunted condos or high-rise buildings here. Only haunted mineral springs spas and 125-year-old libraries. And people in Southern Indiana usually don't encounter their ghosts while they're driving a brand-new sports car. Rather, they're captaining a paddleboat, walking through a railroad tunnel, or driving an old farm pickup truck. The ghosts of Southern Indiana also prefer more traditional modes of transportation, like horses . . . even if, as in one case, the horse is on fire!

Sure, there are a few stories coming out of Southern Indiana that feature technology. It's just rare to find anyone who believes those stories. After all, in Southern Indiana, you're only supposed to believe the old ghost stories. It's tradition.

Will Danny Guthrie Ever Find Peace?

On the morning of May 28, 1991, Daniel "Danny" Guthrie left his house, telling his wife that he was going to spend the day fishing with his friend, Charles Sweeney. The following day, when Guthrie didn't return home, his wife phoned the police. Authorities were dispatched to speak with Sweeney—the last person known to been with Guthrie. Sweeney stated that he and Guthrie had returned from their fishing trip sometime between 4:00 P.M. and 6:00 P.M., and he had not seen Guthrie since. Satisfied with what Sweeney had to say, authorities left his house and continued their investigation.

Nine months later, when the Bureau of Alcohol, Tobacco, and Firearms was investigating an incident in which someone placed a pipe bomb under a local detective's police car, Charles Sweeney's name came up. After being interrogated several times by federal agents, Sweeney finally broke down and agreed to a plea agreement on June 26, 1992. As part of the agreement, Sweeney would plead guilty to placing the bomb under the officer's car and name all the others involved. But there was one other thing that Sweeney agreed to with his plea: to disclose the whereabouts of Danny Guthrie's body.

Sweeney, however, claimed he did not kill Guthrie. Rather, he said that after they returned from their fishing trip, Sweeney agreed to give Guthrie 150 of his marijuana plants in exchange for a saddle. Sweeney pointed Guthrie in the direction of the plants and then left to go play bingo. When Guthrie's wife called the following day and said her husband never came home, Sweeney went out to his marijuana field where he found Guthrie dead from a gunshot wound to the head. Not wanting the authorities to find his marijuana plants, Sweeney said he made the decision to bury Guthrie's body in a ditch and cover it all up with dirt and garbage.

On July 1, 1992, almost fourteen months from the day Danny Guthrie disappeared, police obtained a search warrant for Sweeney's property and recovered the body. It was exactly where Sweeney said it would be. And as Sweeney had stated, Guthrie had been killed by a single shot to the head from a 9mm handgun. Several days later, when forensic techs found that the bullet that killed Guthrie had been fired from a gun owned by Charles Sweeney, he was arrested and charged with murder. Sweeney would be convicted by a jury of his peers and sentenced to sixty years in jail.

After Guthrie's decomposed body was removed from the shallow grave, it was relocated to Henryville's Mt. Zion Cemetery. Although his murderer was discovered, it appears as though Guthrie's spirit does not rest in peace. People visiting his grave have been overcome with icy-cold chills, even on bright, sunny days. A shadowy figure resembling that of a man is also seen standing near Guthrie's grave. Some even claim that they have heard Guthrie himself speaking whenever they come close to his grave.

Even Ghosts Need a Little R and R

When the first settlers came to the area known as French Lick, they discovered that there was an abundance of natural mineral water flowing there. They also learned that as the water rushed over the rocks, it left behind a white residue, which wildlife would come and lick. In a nod to the French fur trappers that were first to this area, it was given the name French Lick.

It would be those natural mineral springs that put French Lick on the map. In 1833, the enterprising Dr. William Bowles bought up roughly fifteen thousand acres around the springs and quickly began promoting and selling bottles of "miracle water." In less than a decade, Bowles had made enough money to build the French Lick Springs Hotel, which he opened in 1845.

The hotel was an immediate success and as word spread about the free-flowing mineral water, more and more people descended on French Lick. In the 1880s and '90s, the hotel was expanded and additional buildings were added to the property. Things really took off, however, when a group of investors, led by Indianapolis mayor Thomas Taggart, bought the hotel in 1901.

Taggart's love affair with the hotel began shortly after his group purchased it. Under his watch, the entire property received a facelift, including the addition of entire new wings. Another popular feature was a championship golf course, the first of what would eventually amount to three at the resort. He added a bottling house for on-site bottling and distribution of the mineral water. He even made sure that people could get in and out of the resort with relative ease, going so far as to have a special railroad spur created that would bring passenger trains right to the front door of the resort. Clearly, Taggart loved the hotel and resort. So is it really that surprising to find that his ghost is still hanging out here?

The one spot in the hotel that offers the best chance of encountering Taggart's ghost is around the service elevator. Smoky white mists are seen here, and people sometimes smell the overpowering odor of pipe or cigar smoke. Apparently, Taggart's ghost is something of a prankster: he is blamed for suddenly closing the service elevator door at the worst possible moments, such as when employees have their hands full or they are in a rush to go to another floor.

In keeping with his playful manner, Taggart's ghost reportedly makes a grand entrance in the ballroom by arriving on top of a ghostly horse!

The Curious History of the West Baden Springs Hotel

Dr. William Bowles started construction on the French Lick Springs Hotel in the 1830s. A decade later in 1846, as Bowles prepared to enlist in the Mexican-American War, he approached a fellow doctor, Dr. John Lane, with a proposition. Bowles wanted Lane to sign a five-year lease with him. Bowles needed someone to look after the hotel while he served in the army. Lane agreed and even though Bowles ended up coming back three years earlier than the term of the lease, Lane had spent enough time there that he made the decision to create his own hotel near the springs. So, in 1851, Lane purchased 770 acres from Bowles and began work on his own hotel.

The following year, the Mile Lick Inn, named for a nearby settlement, opened. Like the French Lick Springs Hotel, the Mile Lick also bottled and distributed mineral water, which helped raise awareness about the inn. Mile Lick also took another page from the French Lick Springs Hotel playbook when it negotiated with the local railroad to have tracks laid out close to the entrance to their resort.

As Mile Lick Hotel continued to draw attention, comparisons to Wiesbaden, Germany, which also relied heavily on its mineral springs, were made. So much so that in 1855, Mile Lick was officially renamed West Baden. Shortly thereafter, the Mile Lick Hotel followed suit and became the West Baden Springs Hotel.

In 1888, a private group purchased the hotel and began making improvements at a mind-boggling pace. They even went so far as to create a two-story, covered, $1/3$-mile bicycle and pony track. And in the center of that was a baseball diamond that was later used for spring training games by teams such as the Cincinnati Reds and the Chicago Cubs.

Over the years, as the hotel continued to grow and prosper, it became the setting for historic events. Between 1918 and 1919, part of the hotel was designated Army Hospital No. 35, where soldiers wounded in World War I were treated. And a famous scene played out at the hotel on the day of the 1929 Stock Market Crash, as employees and wealthy guests, many of whom had made their fortunes in the stock market, gathered together in the hotel's offices awaiting confirmation that the market had indeed crashed. Word finally did arrive and the following morning, almost all of the guests had departed.

Management attempted to keep the hotel open during the Depression, but it became increasingly difficult to keep things running. In an odd move, in 1934, the decision was made to donate the entire property, then valued at more than $6.5 million, to the Jesuits, who turned it into a seminary. For the next thirty years, the Jesuits made significant modifications to the property. They began by turning the hotel lobby into a chapel and installing stained glass windows. A cemetery was added to the property, as well. But one of the boldest moves made was to dump truckload after truckload of rocks into the mineral springs, essentially filling them in. When that was done, concrete caps were placed over all the springs.

After the Jesuits left, the property changed hands several times, and it fell more and more into disrepair with each new owner. Finally, in 1996, Cook Group, Inc., took control and began the painstaking, time-consuming, and costly job of restoring the resort to its former glory. Untold hours of hard labor and literally tens of millions of dollars were sunk into the project, but the result is amazing.

With such a rich history and so many people passing through the resort over the years, it is futile to try to identify the ghosts.

Although cold breezes are felt and phantom footsteps are heard throughout the hotel, it's nearly impossible to put a face to the feelings and sounds.

For example, there is the ghost said to haunt the third floor. When spotted, this apparition is described as a man wearing 1900s-era clothing and a bowler hat. He walks up and down the hallways late at night, apparently oblivious to the fact that the living are standing right next to him.

The second floor of the hotel is where guests have claimed to see strange mists creeping down the hallway. Sometimes pale green lights are sighted.

Heading down to the ground floor, there are reports of a woman in a beautiful gown in the atrium. There might even be a rather cranky ghost in the hotel lobby, as this is where some guests claim to be touched, pushed, and even slapped. And while guests are not permitted in the basement of the hotel, that is where employees have seen shadowy, moving figures resembling human beings.

Finally, there are whispers about the ghosts of two men who committed suicide by jumping from the roof of the hotel after receiving the news that the stock market had crashed that fateful day in 1929. Their ghosts are seen throughout the property, including up on the roof of the hotel, where they allegedly leaped to their deaths.

The Legendary Gray Lady of Willard Library

The Willard Library is the oldest public library in the state of Indiana. Some people say it is the most haunted, too. In fact, many would argue that the Willard Library's Gray Lady is the most well-known of all Hoosier ghosts. That's no small feat, considering that when the library opened in 1885, there were no reports of ghosts, strange noises, or anything out of the ordinary. In fact, more than fifty years passed before the very first ghostly encounter.

In 1937, one of the nighttime maintenance workers descended the library's staircase to check the furnace in the basement. He hadn't been down there long when he encountered what he described as an "all-gray lady" who appeared before him and then vanished. The man was so shaken by what he saw that he quit his job soon after. The legend of the Gray Lady was born.

Since that night in 1937, hundreds of people, from patrons to library staff, have had chance encounters with a mysterious, veiled woman wearing all gray. She is seen throughout the library, during both day and night. There are, however, several places in the library that she seems to prefer. She is most often seen in and around the Children's Room in the library's basement. But in one famous encounter, police responding to the tripping of the library's burglar alarm were shocked and surprised to see a woman dressed in gray staring out at them from one of the building's upstairs windows. Upon entering the library, it was found to be empty.

Just because you can't always see the Gray Lady doesn't mean she isn't there. Books and furniture have been known to move on their own in the library, and bathroom faucets turn themselves on and off—all activity credited to the Gray Lady. There are also random cold spots that float through the library, chilling all those they envelop. Finally, there is the faint odor of perfume that appears and disappears without any source being detected.

Who exactly the Gray Lady is has been puzzling and frustrating researchers and library staff for years. Her gray attire has been dated to the late 1800s, which coincides with the time period when the library first opened. So some believe the Gray Lady was one of the original employees, perhaps a librarian.

In recent years, interest in the Gray Lady has grown, with several ghost reality shows, including Syfy's *Ghost Hunters*, descending on the Willard in an attempt to find her. The library also created a buzz with the launching of not one, but two websites—libraryghost.com and willardghost.com—that allow guests to take part in a ghost hunt from the safety of their own homes by viewing feeds from live video cameras stationed throughout the Willard Library. Guests are even encouraged to do a screen grab and submit any paranormal activity they see. Both sites have submitted photos, some obviously faked, that are alleged to show the Gray Lady roaming the library, both during the day as well as late at night. Take a peek and judge for yourself if you believe there really is a ghost haunting the stacks of the Willard!

Dark Phantom on a Fiery Steed

It's been more than 150 years since a harrowing encounter with a dark phantom occurred on River Road. And yet, the event was so frightening, so disturbing, that it is still talked about today and never fails to deliver a chill up the spine of all who hear it.

In the 1850s, River Road was not only the road of choice for traveling between Tell City and Carmelton, it was the only way to get back and forth between the two towns. So the road was fairly well-traveled and people were familiar with the sights and sounds of the road. Nothing, however, could prepare folks for what they would see on the road one night in 1858.

On a crisp yet sunny afternoon in September 1858, friends and family members gathered together in River Road's Mulberry Park to celebrate the wedding of Amanda Brazee and Paul Schuster. It was a celebration, to be sure, and everyone was in fine spirits. That is, until some of the guests began pointing at something moving off in the distance down River Road.

As more and more guests turned to face River Road to see the mysterious object moving towards them, it soon became clear that it was a rider on horseback. But this was no ordinary rider or horse. When it drew near, guests were horrified to see that the horse appeared to be on fire! As for the rider, most of his features were hidden beneath a long black riding cloak. One hand would occasionally appear from beneath the cloak, brandishing a riding crop with which he urged the horse to run faster and faster.

Some guests began running for cover, while others simply stood, transfixed, as the dark figure on the flaming horse came closer and closer. Just as it reached the point where it would crash headlong into the wedding guests, horse and rider suddenly reared up, turned, and went galloping back down River Road, disappearing into the twilight.

Slowly, the wedding guests came back to their senses and tried to rationalize what they had just seen. Surely, too many of them had seen the horse and rider, so it could not have been a figment of their imaginations. So it must have been real. But what was it? A ghost? A demon? Or perhaps just someone trying out an early Halloween prank? Whatever it was, the guests decided to just forget the incident and get back to the matter at hand: the wedding celebration. But such ghostly visions are not easily forgotten. It didn't help things, either, when several days later, others started having their own horrifying encounters with the dark figure and his fiery steed. In one instance, a man fired shots at the rider, which seemed to have no effect.

As the 1900s dawned and more modern roads began to criss-cross the county, sightings of the horse and rider along River Road began to dwindle.

In the 1940s, a flood wall was erected that essentially cut off the section of River Road where the apparition would appear. And with that, the stories of the dark rider atop a blazing horse stopped. But who's to say what would happen if on some dark night, someone were to peek over the flood wall just to see what they could see?

Purple Head Bridge

Winding your way along Breevort Road, just outside of Vincennes, you'll start to see signs for the Illinois border. What the signs don't tell you is that to cross the state line, you will have to drive over a unique—and some would say haunted—bridge that also has a strange nickname: the Purple Head Bridge.

Originally known as the Wabash Cannonball Bridge, the structure is truly something to behold. It's massive, spanning the Wabash River at a length of more than one thousand feet. It was originally constructed as a one-track railroad bridge in the late 1890s. As time went by the railroad gradually added sections as needed, rather than replacing the whole structure at once, so some portions are still original and others are replacements. Eventually, the upkeep on the bridge became too much and the railroad abandoned it.

In the 1970s, the structure was renamed Stangle's Bridge, after the new owner, Frank Stangle, who purchased the bridge with the intent of turning it into a toll bridge for cars. Apparently not wanting to sink too much money into the bridge, Stangle decided to simply pull up the rails and cover the holes with wood, making for a somewhat bumpy and harrowing ride across the bridge's one lane. The bridge changed hands several more times before it was acquired by the state of Illinois around 2009.

Ask anyone who lives nearby and they will tell you the real name of the structure is Purple Head Bridge. It is unclear when people

began calling it that name, but the moniker stems from the 1750s during the time of the French and Indian War. Though the bridge did not exist back then, the site where it now stands is alleged to have been the location of several bloody skirmishes between Native Americans and settlers.

According to legend, during a battle that took place upstream from the bridge, a local shaman was killed, his body falling into the water. His tribesmen attempted to retrieve their fallen comrade's body, but as the battle raged on, they were forced to watch helplessly as the current pulled his corpse along. The body eventually came to rest in the shallows, where it remained for several days, slowly bloating up and turning a sickly purple. The shaman's tribe made several other attempts to retrieve the body, but without success. Eventually, the body simply floated away.

It is said that because the shaman was never given a proper burial, his spirit is condemned to haunt the spot of his death. For that reason, people brave enough to either walk up onto the bridge or simply stop their car and look out over it have sometimes encountered what appears to be the bloated purple head of the shaman rising up out of the water. The shaman's hands then appear, stretching out as he implores witnesses to help him receive a proper burial. It's hard to say what happens next, though, as most people don't stick around long enough to find out.

The Ghosts of the Big Tunnel of Tunnelton

Almost everyone who visits Tunnelton, Indiana, nestled in Lawrence County, for the first time asks the locals the same question: "So where's the tunnel?" After all, one would assume that with a name like Tunnelton, there's got to be a tunnel somewhere, right? Well, in the case of this tiny town, not only does it deliver with one whopper of a tunnel, but the entire area surrounding it is said to be haunted by more ghosts than you could shake a spectral stick at.

In the 1850s, the Ohio and Mississippi Railroad was laying tracks through the area when they ran into a problem. In front of them was a hill that seemed to be composed almost entirely of limestone.

They were down in a valley with the White River blocking their route in one direction, so the railroad had no choice but to attempt to plow right through the hill. It was rough going, and a few workers are said to have lost their lives in the process, but they eventually made it through to the other side. They had been forced to create a bend in the tunnel, however, and it was so sharp that one is unable to see the other end from the opening. The tunnel itself ended up being nearly eighteen hundred feet long, earning it the title Big Tunnel. In fact, that name is still visible to this day over the entrance.

Today, the tunnel is still used by CSX Transportation, although not many trains make their way along the tracks. But that doesn't mean the tunnel is abandoned. Far from it. In fact, it is a popular travel destination for young and old alike, most of whom are trying to catch a glimpse of the many ghosts said to haunt the tunnel. But just who are these ghosts?

One ghost believed to haunt the site is that of one of the workers killed during the tunnel's construction. Apparently, the man lost his head while working in the tunnel, but his spirit remained. His headless ghost is said to roam the tunnel at night, lantern in hand, searching for his lost head.

There is also a long-standing rumor that during construction the workers were unaware that there was a cemetery on top of the hill they were digging under. As the workers dug, one by one, bodies and caskets from the cemetery fell through the tunnel roof onto the ground, creating a rather rude awakening for some of the spirits who were enjoying their eternal slumber. Most were apparently able to get back to sleep, but a few restless souls never recovered and wander the tunnel. Two ghosts frequently seen are a middle-aged man and a young girl.

The best-known ghost of the Big Tunnel, however, is Henry Dixon. While the events leading up to Dixon's demise are shrouded in mystery, it is clear he was the victim of foul play. Whether or not he was killed inside the tunnel or his body was simply dumped there is unknown, but the killer's intent was that a train would come by and destroy the remains. Dixon's body was actually discovered before a train came through, but there still was not enough evidence to convict anyone and the case remains unsolved to this day. Perhaps that's why Dixon's ghost still hangs out at the tunnel, waiting for justice to finally be served.

Finally, if you walk up the tracks just a short distance from the tunnel, you will find yourself in an area known locally as the Devil's Backbone. It is here that on one dark night, a family was riding along the ridge above the tracks in their horse-drawn carriage. Perhaps something spooked the horses or maybe the driver simply lost control of the carriage. Either way, the entire carriage—family, horses, and all—plunged over the embankment, killing everyone. Today, they say that if you are in the Devil's Backbone on just the right night, you will hear the fatal crash being reenacted. First, you will hear the wild neighing of the horse, followed by a woman's screams, and then children crying. After that, the sounds of something big and heavy reverberate across the hillside. Then all will be silent once again, without a single trace of anything having happened.

"Curse Those Steamboats!"

In the early 1800s, Francis "Frank" McHarry enjoyed a successful venture as a ferryboat captain, shuttling people back and forth across the Ohio River. With the advent of the steamboat, however, Captain McHarry's business began to suffer. Not only that, but he began to secretly despise the steamboats, because he felt their wakes were rocking his own boat. Eventually, McHarry gave up trying to conceal his displeasure and openly mocked and complained about the steamboats. Then, according to legend, McHarry came up with a plan to ensure that he'd be able to poke fun at the steamboats on the Ohio River for years to come, if not for all eternity.

McHarry's plan was to have an enormous mausoleum erected on a bluff overlooking the river. That way, after McHarry shuffled off the mortal coil, his ghost could hang out at the mausoleum and hurl insults down the hill at the steamboats as they passed by below. McHarry immediately started putting his plan into action, and before long, ships passing by one particular hillside just outside of Elizabeth could see the top of a stone mausoleum poking up through the trees.

In 1857, Captain Frank passed away and according to his wishes he was entombed in his hillside mausoleum. As soon as the mausoleum door was closed, friends and family members waited patiently for the next steamboat to slide by on the Ohio River to see if the captain's ghost would make good on his promise. But as the first ships came into view, there was nothing to be heard, either from inside or outside the mausoleum. Perhaps a bit dejected, everyone went home and thought that was the end of that. They were wrong.

Before long, captains and even passengers on boats claimed to have seen strange lights circling around McHarry's mausoleum late at night. Everyone who saw the lights was convinced they belonged to McHarry's ghost.

As time went by, McHarry's relatives and friends began to find the strenuous climb up the hill to the mausoleum to be quite bothersome, if not impossible. So McHarry's body was eventually removed from this tomb and moved to the Cave Hill Cemetery in Louisville, Kentucky, where he shares a mausoleum with his son-in-law, Capt. James E. Irvin and his wife, Frances, who was McHarry's daughter.

As for the spirit of Frank McHarry, it is said to have returned to his old hillside tomb, perhaps to hurl one last insult down at any passing boats he might see. On certain nights, a bright light is sometimes seen moving about the outside of the stone tomb, even though there is no one up there . . . and least not anyone alive.

The Hackler Family's Fire-Safety Demonstration

One morning in April 1941, farmer William Hackler awoke early as he always did and got ready for a long day in the field. By 8:00 A.M., the entire family had awakened, eaten breakfast, and begun preparing to head out to the fields. That's when William Hackler caught a whiff of smoke. Turning, it seemed as though something on the second floor of the house was on fire. While his wife phoned the fire department, Hackler and the rest of the family raced upstairs to see if they could put the fire out. After looking for several minutes without seeing any open flame, the fire department arrived and joined in the search. They eventually found a small fire smoldering inside a wall on the second floor, which they immediately extinguished. The firemen took a look around, but could find no obvious cause. The Hacklers thanked their firemen, bid them farewell, and then got back to their work. But they had barely gotten back out of the house when they once again smelled smoke coming from upstairs. As before, the family took off up the stairs while Mrs. Hackler once again called the fire department.

This time, the fire was found to be coming from a mattress in a spare bedroom on the second floor. The family was perplexed as to how this fire could have started since the bedroom hadn't been used the night before. In fact, no one had even been in the room in the last twenty-four hours. When the firemen arrived for a second time at the Hackler farm, the mystery deepened when they found that the fire had started inside the mattress. Not seeing any rips or tears in the mattress, the firemen decided to take the mattress outside, open it up, and put the fire out that way. One firefighter later said "it was like the fire was completely contained in the mattress—there was no way in the world you could set a fire like that."

As the firemen were once again preparing to take their leave, Mrs. Hackler cried out from inside the house that there was another fire. What happened next was a bizarre game of cat and mouse between the firemen and whatever supernatural force was starting the fires. The firemen would run to one side of the house to put out a fire, only to find that as one was extinguished, another one would break out on the other side of the house. Even more perplexing was how things were burning: books burning from the inside out, a pair of overalls bursting into flames with no one around them, paper wall calendars suddenly smoldering and then disintegrating before everyone's very eyes.

By mid-afternoon, it was estimated that close to thirty separate fires had erupted throughout the Hackler homestead. It took nearly one hundred firemen from three separate divisions to keep the entire house from going up in flames. As night fell, things finally started to quiet down, and except for the overpowering odor of smoke in the air, it appeared as though the worst had passed. The Hacklers, however, weren't taking any chances. Not willing to risk sleeping inside a potential powder keg, but also wanting to make sure the house could be saved should another fire break out, they made the decision to move all the beds out into the front yard and spend the night there.

Thankfully, there were no more fires at the Hackler house, either that night or any other night. The mysterious fires stopped just as suddenly as they had started, with no explanation ever being given as to who, or what, was responsible for starting them all.

As an interesting postscript to this story, a unique ad featuring the mysterious fires at the Hackler homestead began running in both local and national magazines. Travelers' Insurance Company, the Hackler's insurance agency, ran the ads. The ads said that Travelers protects their client from any type of fire, even those caused by a poltergeist!

Fort Wayne
and
Eastern Indiana

FORT WAYNE IS THE SECOND-LARGEST CITY IN INDIANA. IT'S ALSO HOME to one of the largest genealogy collections in the United States, currently housed at the Allen County Public Library. The legendary Johnny Appleseed is buried in Fort Wayne, too. Put that all together and what do you get? A wonderful blend of history and folklore, which is a perfect way to describe the ghost stories associated not only with Fort Wayne, but the entire eastern section of Indiana, too.

Ghost stories coming out of Eastern Indiana tend to be attached to historically significant buildings, such as courthouses, airports, and institutions of higher learning, but they can also be found in tried-and-true locations with foreboding names, like Devil's Hollow, or destinations that are so descriptive that anyone going there will know exactly what to expect, like Blood Road. Mix it all together and you'll see that the ghost stories of Eastern Indiana are doing double duty. They are keeping Indiana history alive while providing people with a nice, healthy dose of chills to boot.

Down in Devil's Hollow

For more than sixty years, generation after generation of teenagers have been making the pilgrimage out Old Auburn Road towards the

DeKalb County line to enter an area known as Devil's Hollow. No, they aren't looking to meet the man in red with the flaming pitchfork. Rather, they are trying to validate a legend about a man, a lantern, and a mysterious message hidden in a fence—no easy task considering the story keeps changing.

The most current version of the story takes place in the early 1940s. In it, a man lives out in Devil's Hollow in a simple house with his wife and eighteen-year-old son. Everything is going well for the family until a letter arrives in the mail, addressed to the son. Opening it, the son learns that he has been drafted by the army and is being called upon to fight overseas. His mother begs him not to go, but the son tells her it is his duty. Several days later, with tears in her eyes, the mother waves goodbye to her son as he heads off to report for duty. As a symbol of her love, the mother promises her son that she will light a lantern and place it in the window every night until he returns.

Flash forward several months. The son is still overseas in Europe while his father and mother hold down the family homestead and await his return. One morning, there is a knock at the door. Opening it, the parents see two men dressed in formal military attire. They know instantly that this cannot be good. And they are correct. Their only son has been killed in battle.

Grief-stricken, the mother loses the will to do anything. Anything, that is, except to faithfully place a lit lantern in the window every night. Her husband implores her to stop, telling her she needs to accept the fact that their son is never coming home. Night after night, like clockwork, however, the mother lights the lantern in the window.

Eventually, because she no longer takes care of herself, the mother gets sick and passes away. Now the father is overcome with grief. For a while, it seems the only thing that helps the man keep his sanity is to carry on his wife's nightly ritual of placing a lit lantern in the front window. But soon, not even that helps. People driving over the old wooden bridge near the family home now notice something different—the father has been fashioning a fence around the property using tree limbs from the woods. Each time they go by, the people see more and more of the fence in place. And then strange symbols start appearing on the posts, apparently carved in by the father.

One night, the father finally snaps. He walks out to the wooden bridge, wraps a noose around his neck, and hangs himself from the bridge. When his body is discovered the following morning, people go up to the family home to see if they can find anything that can help explain this senseless and tragic loss of life. Looking around the house, they find everything seems to be in order. The only thing odd is the still-burning lantern in the front window. They search for a suicide note, but the closest thing they find is a single piece of paper on the kitchen table, stating simply "read the fence." The note is in the man's handwriting.

Walking out to the front yard, everyone looks at the weird symbols carved into the fences. If there is a message hidden within the symbols, they are unable to figure it out.

It is said that if you make your way out to the old bridge, you will see a single light coming from the woods. It appears to be the light from a lantern, even though the family home was torn down years ago. Also, if you listen closely, you will hear sobbing coming from under the bridge—the mournful cries of a man who tried for as long as he could to keep his family together.

Today, the Internet is abuzz with people trying to get directions to this location. It doesn't help that the area has changed significantly since the story first started making the rounds. Even the wooden bridge that used to cross Cedar Creek and was a focal point of this story has been torn down, replaced by a more modern one. But still they come. Proving once and for all that a good ghost story never dies . . . it just mutates every few years.

The Wild Woman of Christy Woods

Named after former Ball State University faculty member Dr. Otto Christy, Christy Woods is an eighteen-acre property that runs between Tillotson and Riverside Avenues in Muncie. Used mainly as an outdoor classroom for Ball State, the woods have numerous trails running throughout them, used by both students and joggers. Ask anyone who has ever had the opportunity to take a stroll through the grounds of the woods and they will tell you it's a truly wonderful place. That is, of course, until you head over to the southern end of the property, where things get a little creepy.

The reason the creep factor tends to run so high in the southern end of the woods is because this is where, if you believe the stories, a disturbing ghostly girl likes to hang out. No one is sure who this ghost is or what caused her to take up residence in Christy Woods. But one look at this girl and you'll know, whatever happened, it wasn't pretty. That's because this girl is described as having wild, matted hair and ripped clothing. Most people who have seen her say it looks as though she has just been attacked. A few people, mistaking the ghost for a real-life girl, have attempted to help her, only to see her vanish.

Amelia Earhart Is Still Hanging Out at the Airport

In 1932, Amelia Earhart became the first woman to make a solo flight over the Atlantic Ocean. She quickly flew into the hearts of Americans everywhere. To capitalize on that, as well as create excitement for her next endeavor, a solo flight around the world, Earhart set out touring the country, making appearances and giving speeches. In the fall of 1935, Earhart spoke at Purdue University, and staff were so impressed with her that they offered her a position as a visiting faculty member in the Women's Career Department, which she graciously accepted.

For the next two years, Earhart worked at the university while training for her attempt to fly around the world. To train, she was given access to Hangar 1 at Purdue University Airport. In addition, the university, using money collected through donations, was able to purchase a Lockheed 10E Electra that Earhart used for training. It was not uncommon to see the plane, with Earhart at the controls, flying over the university in the mid-afternoon sun.

In March 1937, using the Lockheed 10E Electra given to her by the school, Earhart and her navigator, Fred Noonan, made their first attempt to fly around the world. Technical difficulties forced them to scrap the attempt until June. They made it as far as New Guinea. On the morning of July 2, they took off from that location and were never heard from again.

No trace of the plane ever surfaced—at least not in physical form, anyway. Legend has it that Earhart's ghost has returned to

Hangar 1 at Purdue University Airport, where she spent so much time preparing for her fateful flight. Not content to hide in the shadows, the encounters with Earhart's ghost inside the hangar have been so real as to make people believe they were seeing a flesh-and-blood woman rather than a ghost. Airport security guards have even been convinced that they are dealing with a prowler or thief as they chase after Earhart's ghost, only to have her vanish right before their very eyes. In one instance, a security guard even took a shot at Earhart's ghost when it refused his orders to stop. The bullet had absolutely no effect.

Bud Berger, Eternal Stage Manager

The theater now known as the Embassy in Fort Wayne opened for the first time on May 14, 1928, under the name the Emboyd Theatre. In addition to the fact that the theater was literally in the middle of the seven-story Indiana Hotel, the truly unique part of the Emboyd was the theater's Grande Page pipe organ, with more than eleven hundred pipes. And as the theater's very first stage manager, Bud Berger was there to see it all and loved it. It's been said that if there ever was a man who was destined to work in a theater, it was Bud. It didn't matter how menial or boring the task at hand was, if it involved the theater, Bud was all over it and did it with a smile on his face. It got to the point where Bud actually felt sad when he had to leave the theater at the end of his shift. So when Bud rationalized with his bosses that if he were allowed to live in the theater's basement, he could keep a closer eye on things, they agreed. Bud was overjoyed. Now, he would never have to leave the place that he loved so much.

Over the years, things changed at the theater. Live theater gave way to movies (and then this later reversed again). Employees came and went. Even the name of the building changed from the Emboyd to the Embassy. Through it all, there were only two constants: the Grande Page pipe organ and Bud Berger. To Bud, it didn't matter who was running the show or what kind of show it was. As long as he was part of it, that was fine with him. In 1965, though, the final curtain fell on Bud Berger's life when he passed away. But as anyone involved in the theater business will tell you, once it's in your blood, it's there forever. So to the surprise of no one, Bud Berger decided to hang around the Embassy and take a couple of curtain calls.

Since his passing, Bud Berger's ghost has become something of a guardian angel for the Embassy. It's almost as though he's still watching over it, much the same way he did when he was alive. Several times, the Embassy has fallen on hard times. At one point in 1972, the theater was scheduled for the wrecking ball. But each time, right before things got really bad, the Embassy's luck changed and something happened to save it. That, Embassy employees will tell you, is no coincidence. It's Bud.

But Bud Berger's ghost doesn't always hide in the shadows. Sometimes, he even comes out and takes center stage . . . even if you can't see him. Actors and Embassy employees alike have been taken aback when they inadvertently walk into a freezing cold spot on the stage. That cold spot, they will tell you, is Bud.

Other times, seats in the theater will move up and down on their own. And if someone is on stage practicing or setting something up, a single seat will move down, stay that way for a while, and then slowly move back up. It's almost as if someone unseen came into the theater, sat down for a while, and then got back up and left. Again, they will tell you that Bud is responsible.

Finally, late at night after the show's over and everyone has packed up and headed home, a few people lingering behind in the darkened theater will hear the Grande Page pipe organ begin to play on its own, without anyone being around it. And who do you think they'll say is responsible for that?

Rocking Your Ghost to Sleep

Laurel was one of the many towns that sprang to life in the 1830s with the arrival of the canal systems to Indiana. When Squires Clements made the decision to erect an inn in Laurel, he couldn't have picked a better spot than the corner of Franklin and Baltimore Streets, because it was so close to the canal. When he opened up his White Hall Tavern for business, offering hot meals, cold drinks, and a place to stay the night, Clements knew he was on to something. All he needed to do was sit back, wait for a boat to pull up to the dock, and then unlock the door to his tavern and rake in the money.

One morning, though, something different showed up at the tavern's door. It was a young woman, heavy with child. With her baby due any moment, the woman was trying to get to her husband, who had taken a job out west. The woman, however, had become ill and too weak to carry on. Squires and his wife took pity on the woman and allowed her to spend the night at the tavern. It was their plan that perhaps after a good night's sleep and a good meal, the woman might be strong enough to continue her journey west.

That night, though, the woman went into labor and gave birth inside the White Hall Tavern. At that point, it was evident that for the time being, she was not going to be able to go anywhere. So the following morning, Mrs. Clements told the boat captain to continue on without the woman and to let the woman's husband know where he could find his wife and new child.

When Mrs. Clements returned to the tavern to check on the mother and the baby, she became concerned. The child appeared sickly and the mother did not look much better. Mrs. Clements did what she could and reassured the woman that she could stay at the tavern as long as she needed to.

That night, as the Clements were asleep in bed, they were suddenly awakened by the sound of a baby crying. As they listened, they heard the mother walk across the floor, apparently to go pick the child up. Then they heard the sound of a rocking chair slowly creaking back and forth as the mother tried to rock her newborn child back to sleep. Throughout the night, the Clements heard the baby cry. Always, after that, they heard the creaking of a rocking chair moving back and forth across the floor.

The next day, Mrs. Clements went in to check on the mother and baby. Moments later, Squires heard his wife cry out. Both mother and child were in the rocking chair, dead, with the baby still in its mother's arms. They had apparently both passed away during the night. Heartbroken, Mr. and Mrs. Clements had mother and child laid to rest near the tavern. As for the woman's husband, he never showed up at the tavern. And some would say his wife and baby never left.

For years after the unfortunate incident, people spending the night at the tavern have asked who the baby belonged to. They asked because they could hear the sound of a baby crying late at night, followed by the sound of someone sitting in a rocking chair and slowly rocking the baby back to sleep.

After the passing of both the Clements, the tavern fell on hard times and was eventually closed down. In 2005, the building suffered extreme fire damage, but it still stands today. But without the ability to spend the night there, it is impossible to say if the ghost of the young woman and her baby are still there or if they were finally able to move on.

Something's Going On Upstairs

Originally constructed as an all-men's dorm in 1938, Elliott Hall is today the smallest dorm on the Ball State University campus. It is also said to be the most haunted. The ghost that is haunting Elliot Hall is that of William Schanberg. A World War II veteran, William enrolled at Ball State in 1946 because of the G.I. Bill.

Legend states that while William was serving his country, his face was horribly burned, resulting in scars that made him extremely self-conscious. In fact, William found it so difficult to mingle with other students that he ended up spending most of his free time alone up in the library on Elliott Hall's fourth floor.

One night in January 1947, William decided he couldn't stand being alone anymore. Filled with despair, threw a rope over one of the exposed rafters in the library. He then dragged a table across the floor, climbed up on top of it, slipped the rope around his neck, and hanged himself.

Even though it's been more than sixty years since that fateful night, Elliott Hall residents still hear the event being played out over and over. Students in the third-floor dorm rooms have heard what sounds like heavy furniture sliding across the ceiling, as if someone is pushing a table around in the library. But when they go up to investigate, the library is empty and nothing has been disturbed. A single staircase is the only access to the library on the north side of the building, and strange occurrences continue even though no one is seen going up or down those stairs. Some students working up in the library late at night have reported seeing a shadowy figure out of the corner of their eye, but when they turn to look, there's no one there.

The Courthouse Ghosts

You would think that having two giant trees growing on its roof would be the weirdest thing about the Greensburg Courthouse. Not so! Although the trees certainly are weird, they can't hold a candle to the ghostly activity said to be going on in the courthouse's basement. It's so wild that I've been told ghosts from the neighborhood have been known to stop by just to see what all the fuss is about.

Construction on the Greensburg Courthouse, located at 150 Courthouse Square in downtown Greensburg, began in early 1874 and was completed before the end of the same year. There are no reports of anything going bump in the night inside the courthouse prior to 1895, leading many to point to an event that year that might be the cause for at least some of the paranormal activity taking place inside the building.

One morning in 1895, as the day janitor was just showing up for work, he found the night janitor, Jack Thompson, lying dead at the bottom of the basement stairs. An examination of the body revealed a broken neck and trauma to the head. With nothing else to go on, Thompson's death was ruled an accident. And that's when the activity began.

Even today, there are reports of weird stuff going on in the courthouse basement. Loud banging noises, like something falling down the stairs, along with footsteps, have been heard coming from the stairwell. People walking on the stairs will suddenly feel cold breezes rushing past them. Or if they are walking up the stairs, they will be overcome with the feeling that someone or something is standing in the basement, looking at them, but when they turn around, there's no one there. Objects in the basement, especially tools, move around from place to place. Could it be, as more than one person has suggested to me, that Thompson is still carrying on his janitorial duties from beyond the grave?

But Thompson's ghost is not the only one believed to have taken up residence at the Greensburg Courthouse. A woman dressed in 1920s clothing joins him. Like Thompson's ghost, this female specter tends to stay in one specific area of the building, but unlike Thompson's ghost, the woman likes to hang out on the courthouse's second floor, where she looks out the window at the people passing by. Interestingly enough, people both inside and outside the courthouse have seen this ghost. But while she does not react to anyone standing outside, when people inside the courthouse approach her, she simply smiles and fades away.

There is one final ghost who might be responsible for some of the ghost activity typically credited to (blamed on) the ghost of Jack Thompson. This ghost, however, doesn't have any ties to the courthouse. So if he's here, he must have just wandered over to join in the ghostly fun.

This ghost is said to belong to a man who fell victim to some mob justice back in 1879. Acquitted of murder in the past, this man was arrested again on a separate charge. He knew the ropes, or thought he did. As he sat in the county jail, located a block or so from the Greensburg Courthouse, a mob assembled outside, with their own sort of rough justice in mind. Without warning, the angry mob stormed the jail, dragged the man from his cell, and promptly hanged him from a tree right outside the jail. The man's restless spirit now walks the street, down to the courthouse.

Blood on the Road

You know how when you were little your parents would always be telling you to make sure your seat belt was on? And that no matter how many times they told you, you kept trying to wriggle out? Well, perhaps if you had heard this story about a little county road near Dunkirk, you would have made it a point to stay buckled in at all times!

As the story goes, a man and his young son once lived on a small farm along County Road 700, a small gravel road outside Dunkirk, near the border of Jay and Delaware Counties. Back in those days, people didn't make a big deal about riding in the back of open trucks. And the farmer's son loved to do just that, especially at the end of a long, hard day working in the fields. Only problem was the son also liked jumping out of the bed of the truck whenever it came to a stop or even slowed down. The farmer kept warning the son that if he didn't stop, he could get hurt or even killed. Still, the boy kept leaping from the back of the truck until the farmer felt the need to do something harsh. He fashioned a seatbelt of sorts out of a long length of chain and bolted one end of it to the bed of the truck. The other end he wrapped around the boy.

After a quick test, the farmer was satisfied that the chain would hold the boy in place, and he set off for home from the fields one night down CR 700. The chain, however, was quite a bit longer than the farmer realized, allowing the son to move all the way to the end of the truck bed. As the farmer continued down the road, the truck hit a bump in the road, which threw the boy from the truck onto the road. It was at this point that the very chain designed to protect the boy became a death trap. Unable to escape the chain, the poor boy was dragged down the length of CR 700. All the while, the boy's father kept driving, oblivious that he was dragging his now-lifeless son's body. When the farmer finally stopped at his destination and went to get his boy from the bed of the truck, he was shocked and horrified to find the bed empty and a long, bloody chain lying on the road. Nearby was his son's dead body. They say that one look at his son's crumbled body was all it took to drive the poor farmer insane.

As horrible as this story is, it doesn't end there. Immediately after the accident, people started avoiding CR 700. They wanted to forget all about the horrible tragedy that took place there and avoid seeing the long, thin line of dried blood than ran down the center of the road, beginning immediately after the bump. Rains came and most thought the blood would wash away. But they were wrong. For a while, the gravel road appeared to be clean, but people driving down it at night reported seeing the long, bloody, red line in front of their headlights as soon as they went over one bump in particular. Worse, this trail of blood was only visible when traveling east, as if one was retracing the path of the young boy on that fateful night when he fell from his father's truck.

Years went by and CR 700 was finally paved over. Many thought this would finally put an end to the mysterious ghostly trail of blood. Once again, they were wrong. Before long, the blood once again appeared in the road, almost as if it had seeped through the pavement. To this day, despite all attempts to eradicate the stains, they still appear. It's almost as if the young boy's ghost is warning everyone who goes down CR 700 to be careful, lest they end up like him.

Cries in the Night

The setting for another variation on the classic crybaby bridge story is a now-closed section of Heacock Road in Dublin. This story opens with a young mother driving with her newborn baby in a pickup truck, attempting to get home in a sudden rainstorm. It was a moonless night and with buckets of rain coming down on this isolated stretch of road, it was nearly impossible to see even a foot in front of the truck's headlights. Suddenly, the side of the bridge over Symons Creek came looming up in the headlights. The woman realized too late that in the darkness, her pickup truck had drifted off to the right. She attempted unsuccessfully to get control of the vehicle, and the pickup truck, mother, and baby all went crashing down into the water.

With the rain and the darkness, and little traffic passing by, the pickup truck sat in the creek for a long time before being discovered. When rescue workers climbed down and peeked inside, they found the mother, still behind the wheel, dead. The only other items found in the pickup were a baby's blanket and a pacifier. No sign of the baby was ever found.

Local legend holds that if you drive your car down Heacock Road, you will see the figure of a woman, slowly walking on the bridge, looking out into the water. The woman also appears to be crying, but she is not to be fooled with. One couple drove up to the woman and asked if she needed help, only to have her turn and start scratching on the hood and trunk of the car. The couple peeled out and quickly left the area. They lived several miles away, and by the time they arrived back home, they had successfully convinced each other that they had imagined the ghostly woman on the bridge attacking their car. That is, until they looked at the car and found deep scratches, like claw marks, on the hood and trunk.

It should be noted that in recent years the bridge has been torn down and the section of Heacock Road that the bridge was on has been closed off at each end. So there's no way of telling if the woman is still down there, looking for her lost baby.

Fort Wayne's Ever-Elusive Lady in White

One of the oldest and best-known ghost stories from Fort Wayne is also one of the oddest that you'll ever hear. That's because it features a ghost as the subject of police surveillance and even a chase through the streets of downtown.

This story begins in the 1800s and has as its main character a lady dressed in white. But unlike the stereotypical Ladies in White from urban legends who spend most of their time standing motionless in fields or alongside bridges, Fort Wayne's Lady in White was quite the nimble spirit.

It all began when people noticed an odd woman with long hair wearing a white dress walking the streets of downtown and heading towards the Main Street Bridge. The woman appeared so strange to everyone, because as she walked she paid no attention to her surroundings. As more and more people watched this woman, she walked up onto the bridge and then promptly disappeared. Fearing that they had just watched a poor soul end her life by jumping from the bridge, the witnesses summoned the police. They conducted a thorough search of the area, including poking around in the water, but found nothing.

Several nights later, the woman was once again spotted. As she did the previous time, she walked onto the Main Street Bridge and disappeared. Once again, police were unable to find a trace of her and started to think that maybe someone was having a bit of fun at their expense. Their suspicions grew the next time the woman was seen, because this time she was riding in a buggy pulled by two out-of-control horses. That's when the police had decided they'd had enough and made the decision to keep the area under constant surveillance. Ghost or not, the next time this Lady in White showed up, police were going to find out once and for all what exactly was going on.

The police got their chance several nights later. Almost on cue, the Lady in White appeared and started heading towards the bridge. This time, the cops were ready. As they moved in to corner her, the Lady in White suddenly bolted and attempted to elude them. She ducked into an alleyway along College Street with several officers hot on her heels. Once inside the alley, one of the officers produced a blanket, which he threw over the Lady in White's head. The police thought they had finally captured the culprit until they lifted the blanket and found absolutely nothing underneath it! The Lady in White had vanished into thin air.

After that wild police chase, sightings of the Lady in White stopped almost immediately. People surmised that perhaps she had not been a ghost after all, but some poor street person who had either been captured by the police in secret or else decided she'd had enough excitement and moved on to the next town. Both theories were certainly plausible. Only one problem: While these events took place in the 1800s, even today, from time to time, someone will report catching a glimpse of an odd-looking woman wearing a white dress and walking slowly towards Fort Wayne's Main Street Bridge.

Terre Haute
and
Western Indiana

THERE IS A LONG-STANDING THEORY THAT GHOSTS CAN'T CROSS WATER. That notion has even made it into a lot of movies and books. Ever wonder why the Headless Horseman chucked his pumpkinhead at Ichabod instead of just chasing him down? He couldn't cross the bridge over the creek.

The reasons given as to why ghosts can't cross water are usually pretty vague and, to be honest, I was never really convinced that theory was true. If they couldn't cross water, how do all these ghostly pirates get around? But if the theory is true, it might help explain why there are so many ghosts hanging around in Western Indiana: The Mighty Wabash won't let them go!

While the 503-mile-long Wabash River enters Indiana in the northern part of the state, a vast portion of it runs along the western part, essentially forming the Indiana-Illinois border. It even separates Terre Haute from West Terre Haute. If you were to plot all of the reported ghost sightings in Indiana on a map, you'll find large clusters of them are centered in the western part of the state, with multiple haunted locations in a single town. Could it be that the Wabash River is keeping these ghosts here?

Shades of Death

Waveland Shades State Park, located near Waveland, consists of more than three thousand acres sprawling over three counties and has everything you'd want from a state park: hiking trails, camping facilities, picnic areas, and even canoeing. But as you walk through the park and see all the happy, smiling faces, you can't help but wonder if those smiles would fade, even just a little, it they knew that the area was originally known as the Shades of Death.

As hard as it may be to believe, the area really was called Shades of Death, although the reasons why are unclear. But it was already known by that name when James W. Frisz purchased the property in the late 1800s. Frisz believed the name came from the way that the dense trees blocked most of the sunlight out, making it appear to people walking through the area that it was dead. Most people weren't buying it, though, and had their own explanations regarding the odd name.

Some claimed that the woods were the site of a bloody battle between two warring Indian tribes. For hours on end, more than six hundred Indians attacked each other, often resorting to hand-to-hand combat. When it was all over, only twelve men were left alive. As the surviving Indians crawled back to their respective camps and told their fellow tribesmen what had happened, they all became convinced that the woods were cursed and should be avoided at all costs, especially because they were more than likely now haunted by the warriors who had fallen that day in battle. When settlers moved into the area years later, they heard the stories of the bloody fight and therefore called the woods Shades of Death.

Another version of how the name came to be involves a couple who moved to the area and decided to build a home in the middle of the woods. Apparently, the man was a bit of a drunk and an angry one at that. Sadly, the object of all his rage usually ended up being his poor wife. One night, though, the wife decided she had had enough and decided to put an end to her husband's abuse—by burying an ax in his head.

The wife made no attempt to hide what she had done and instead went immediately to her neighbors' house to let them know what had happened. But her neighbors all agreed that the abusive husband had it coming and that what had taken place was justifiable homicide. So they all banded together, buried the dead husband in the woods, and made a promise not to tell anyone else what had happened.

Of course, people will talk and eventually the truth came out. And the name Shades of Death was attached to the woods. History does not record what became of the wife and if she was ever brought up on charges. As for the husband, his body is still supposed to be buried somewhere in the park, possibly explaining why there are reports of a ghostly man with an ax roaming through the woods at night. Thankfully, for the sake of all involved, the ax is in the man's hands, not embedded in his head.

In the 1940s, when Frisz was trying to turn the area into a state park, he decided to shorten the name to the less-foreboding Shades and launched a campaign to "Save the Shades." The response was overwhelming, resulting in the Shades State Park we've all come to know and love.

The Cromwell Cross

It's been my experience that no matter how strange or how unbelievable a ghost story might seem to be, there always ends up being a kernel of truth to the tale. It's as if the story literally mutates over time as it is handed down from person to person or generation to generation. Such is the case of a famous ghost story concerning a dormitory on the campus of Terre Haute's Indiana State University and a ghostly white cross that's visible on the building itself.

Cromwell Hall, named after Terre Haute businessman Beecher Cromwell, was dedicated on November 1, 1964. All was well for a few decades, but then a strange story started making its way across campus. As the story went, a student living on the twelfth floor of Cromwell Hall became incredibly depressed and chose to end his life by jumping out his dorm room window. Soon after, a ghostly white cross appeared under the boy's window, perhaps signaling the return of the boy's spirit to the hall. Soon, people began to hear strange noises and footsteps inside the boy's former room, Number 1221, as well as up and down the hallways on the twelfth floor.

To prove this ghost story was true, students relating the tale always made sure they were telling it in broad daylight in the shadow of Cromwell Hall. When they reached the end, they simply turned and pointed towards the twelfth floor of the dorm. Sure enough, clearly visible on the red bricks underneath one of windows is a white cross.

Now, skeptics will tell you that the cross was put up there on purpose and was not the result of any supernatural activity. To that end, they would be correct. But a young man really did commit suicide by jumping from that very window. The cross was placed under his window as a type of memorial to him.

Of course, all this does nothing to explain the ghostly activity said to take place in and around the young man's former dorm room. Take a poll of Cromwell Hall residents, both past and present, and you'll find that just as many of them have had paranormal encounters as those who say there's nothing at all going on inside the building.

One Last Phone Call

In today's fast-paced society, it's hard to find anyone who goes somewhere without their cell phone. Of course, it wasn't always like that. Perhaps that's what makes the tale of Martin Sheets so intriguing. For he was a man who went to extremes in order to ensure that he'd always be able to reach out and touch someone . . . even if that meant he'd be making that phone call from beyond the grave!

Born on September 11, 1853, near Terre Haute, Martin Alonzo Sheets quickly began making a name for himself as a businessman. It seemed from an early age that anything he got involved with was a success. In the early 1900s, Sheets left Indiana to dabble in the Texas oil industry, returning years later to the Hoosier State as a very wealthy man.

But all was not as perfect as it may have seemed. Shortly after Martin erected a very stately family mausoleum in Terre Haute's Highland Lawn Cemetery, his thirteen-month-old daughter, Ethel, passed away unexpectedly. Soon, Martin began discussing his own final arrangements with his wife, Susan. It was around this time when people first started to notice the businessman acting a bit strangely.

By far, the oddest thing Sheets did was to walk into the local Indiana Bell Telephone Company's office and discuss the logistics of having an actual working telephone placed inside the Sheets Mausoleum. While some stated that Sheets was simply being overly cautious, others began to whisper that the man had developed an acute fear of somehow being buried alive. Before long, rumors began circulating that Sheets was adding things like a rocking chair and even a bottle of whiskey to the inside of his mausoleum. Some said Sheets was even working with the local funeral home to ensure that his casket had special latches fitted on the inside. Apparently, the plan was that if Sheets somehow managed to get buried alive, he'd be able to free himself from the casket, call for help, and then pour himself a strong one as he sat in his rocking chair waiting for help to arrive. Whether or not all of that was true, a telephone pole was eventually erected outside the Sheets mausoleum and phone wires were run down through the wall and a phone was installed. So if Sheets wanted to make his phone call, he was all set.

Obviously, when Sheets passed away in 1926 and was interred, telephone operators began nervously looking at one particular light on their switchboard—the one indicating that a call was coming from inside the mausoleum. Minutes and then hours passed without the light ever coming on. Before long, the operators all breathed a collective sigh of relief and went on about their business.

Days and weeks rolled into months and then years with nary a flicker coming from the "Sheets Light" on the switchboard. Most people began to believe the phone inside the mausoleum was never going to be used. Several years after Sheets died, his wife, Susan, passed away. She was found on the kitchen floor of her family home, the victim of what appeared to be a massive stroke. In her hand, she was still clutching the receiver from the kitchen phone, indicating she died while trying to make a final call for help.

Or was she? Several days later, when the door to the Sheets Mausoleum was once again swung open so that Susan could be laid to rest beside her husband, everything seemed to be in order . . . save for one small thing. The mausoleum phone was off the hook.

So did Martin Sheets decide to make one last phone call to his wife, many years after he died? There are only two people in the world who can answer that question with any certainty. And they are lying peacefully beside each other in Highland Lawn Cemetery. As for the phone line, several years ago, the telephone company decided to finally disconnect the line and remove the telephone pole, just in case Mr. and Mrs. Sheets got any bright ideas and decided to make a bunch of long-distance calls.

Entering Hell's Gate

Indiana is known for having more interstate highway per square mile than any other state, wonderful covered bridges, and of course the Indianapolis 500. The one thing that tends to get overlooked is that Indiana is home to a portal to hell!

Known locally as Hell's Gate, this structure is actually a small tunnel for cars to pass under a set of train tracks in the tiny town of Diamond, just outside Brazil. According to legend, Hell's Gate is haunted, the result of a train derailment that sent railcars tumbling down the embankment, killing many people in the process. It is said that all it takes for a ghostly encounter is to be at the tunnel at just the right time and you will hear the accident playing out before your very ears. If you stop your car in the middle of the tunnel at night, you can hear screams, followed by a loud crashing sound, after which you will hear moans and cries of agony.

As creepy a story as that is, it certainly doesn't explain why the tunnel is referred to as Hell's Gate. That name came about because of another legend that developed concerning not only this tunnel, but the surrounding area as well.

This legend says that the tunnel is an actual gateway to hell, and one of seven gates in and around Brazil. For a ghoulishly good time, simply pull into the tunnel, turn your car off, kill the lights, and wait. (Warning: You are essentially parking in the middle of a public road, which is not recommended.) After sitting there quietly for about ten minutes, the layers of graffiti that litter almost every square inch of the tunnel are supposed to start glowing and blood will start running down the walls. As hard as it might be, keep an eye out for your own name written on the tunnel walls. If you see it, you've been "marked" and you can expect some invisible force to start banging on your car, signifying that it's probably best that you leave.

Oh, and one last thing: If you see your name on the tunnel wall, that's supposed to be a sign that you are going to die soon. Of course, that's the sort of thing that urban legends are made of. Still, it's something to consider before you go planning a trip out to Hell's Gate. After all, there's no sense in tempting fate unnecessarily.

Still Searching for Rebecca's Head

In this well-known tale, a farmer by the name of Lawry lived on the outskirts of Brazil, Indiana, with his daughter, Rebecca. One day in October 1894, Rebecca took a horse and buggy into town to run errands. Her father stayed at home. When darkness fell, Lawry was only mildly concerned that Rebecca hadn't returned yet. He knew that she had a lot of things to take care of in town, so he didn't worry too much. But when a thunderstorm rolled in and started dumping buckets of rain on the area and there was still no sign of her, Lawry walked out onto the front porch and strained his eyes to see if she could be spotted returning in the distance. Minutes later, when a familiar horse and buggy came rolling down towards the house, Lawry let out a sigh of relief, followed by a gasp of horror when he realized the buggy was empty. Snatching up a lantern, Lawry began to wander through the darkness, looking for his daughter.

After Lawry climbed up and down several hills, his lantern shone on a dark mass lying underneath a tree. As he drew nearer, the father realized he was looking at the decapitated body of Rebecca.

They say that after he buried his daughter, Lawry was never quite the same. He still attempted to tend his fields, but now he spent most of his free time wandering the countryside at night with a lantern in his hand. Some said he was looking for Rebecca's killer and others more morbid thought he was looking for her head. Whatever he was looking for, Lawry went to his grave without finding it. Perhaps that is why his ghost is said to still inhabit the area.

It is said that if you go to the area that was once Lawry's property and flash your headlights three times, Lawry's ghost, lantern still in hand, will appear off in the distance and begin searching the woods. In some instances, people see Lawry's full form; at other times only the faint light from his lantern is visible.

Counting the Cemetery Steps

It's officially known as Carpenter's Cemetery, but locals all know it as the 100 Steps Cemetery. It's said to be the place to go if you have a morbid curiosity regarding how you will die. But a word of caution before you go: Make sure you bone up on your counting skills. Otherwise, your demise might come a lot sooner than you think!

As you wind your way along County Road 675 West outside of Brazil, you'd be forgiven if you didn't let out a tiny gasp when you come around a particularly sharp bend in the road. That's because, sitting alongside the road and literally constructed up the side of a hill, is what is known as 100 Steps Cemetery. The name comes from the stone steps that go from the road up the hill to the top of the cemetery. Along the way, there are tombstones, some of which are leaning or have already toppled to the ground, dotting the hill on either side of the steps. Upon reaching the top of the hill, there are several tombstones, all of which overlook a field. This point is referred to as the center of the cemetery.

The legend surrounding this cemetery is one that should be approached with caution. It is said that you must go out to the cemetery at night (in some cases, it must be at midnight). When you arrive at the cemetery, you must stand at the bottom of the steps and then slowly ascend them one at a time, counting them as you go. Once you have reached the top, make sure to face the open field and wait. Eventually, the ghost of the first caretaker of the cemetery will appear and come towards you. When he reaches you, if you haven't already bolted, he will show you a vision that will reveal how you will die. Then, his task being complete, the ghostly caretaker will vanish before your very eyes. Then comes the tricky part.

Once you've recovered from seeing the vision of your death, you must turn and walk back down the steps, once again counting as you go. When you hit the bottom, if you end up with the same number of steps that you counted on the way up, you're home free. But, if you unfortunately end up with a different number, you might want to make a couple of phone calls. That's because you're going to die the way the caretaker foretold that very night. Oh, and just in case after seeing the caretaker's vision, you get the bright idea of trying to forego the step-counting by climbing down the hillside itself, think again. Those who have tried report being shoved to the

ground by unseen hands, so hard that it left red marks on their backs that did not fade away for several weeks.

If you're still thinking you are up for the challenge, here's one final word of caution. It is said that the caretaker, or some other playful ghost, likes to make some of the steps magically vanish, making it quite hard to determine just how many steps there are. Case in point, while it is known as the 100 Steps Cemetery, very few people have ever been able to count more than sixty-five steps.

Still on Patrol After All This Time

As a general rule, cemeteries in the United States close at dusk and do not open again until dawn. Sadly, with the resurgence of ghost hunting comes an increased number of people who feel the need to go into cemeteries at night simply to vandalize. In order to counteract that, more and more police departments are having their officers patrol cemeteries. So if you don't want to risk a ticket or possible arrest, you should stay out of cemeteries at night. And in the case of Putnam County's Boone Hutcheson Cemetery, you just might encounter a police officer who has been dead for more than sixty years.

Created in 1812, Boone Hutcheson Cemetery, or "Boone Hutch," is a beautiful cemetery that sits atop a hillside off of South County Road 450 West. It's the kind of peaceful cemetery where you can take a leisurely stroll and collect your thoughts. Perhaps that's why, if the legend is to be believed, one police officer in particular has chosen to hang around and protect it.

The ghostly officer is said to make his presence known by appearing as a bright blue light that originates at the back of the cemetery. Other times, the officer can be plainly seen and is either bathed in a blue glow or else is carrying a blue light with him. Either way, if he catches you in the cemetery after dark, he's not going to be happy.

If you're not put off by the idea of encountering a police officer from the other side, then how about a pack of spectral dogs with glowing red eyes? That's right, there's supposed to be a group of demonic dogs roaming the cemetery at night, chasing out trespassers who enter the grounds. If you encounter them, you'd better hope you have your running shoes on, because they are rumored to be very, very fast.

One last legend surrounding Boone Hutch is that there is a cave entrance, guarded by a ghost only referred to as a "dark shape." If you manage to get past this creature and enter the cave, you will find that it runs under the cemetery. But be forewarned: According to legend, some of the caskets from the cemetery's "residents" have broken through the roof of the cave and human remains are said to be scattered about. So there's no telling what, or who, you might be crawling over if you enter the cave.

Pennies for Pearl

Early on the morning of Saturday, February 1, 1896, the body of an unidentified young woman was found lying on a piece of farmland in Fort Thomas, Kentucky. The body was headless and lacked identification. It was only after noticing that the woman's shoes bore the stamp of a Greencastle, Indiana, store that the body was identified as that of twenty-two-year-old Pearl Bryan, who lived in Greencastle. Once authorities knew who the victim was, they began looking into her history to see if they could find the killer.

It didn't take long for authorities to show up on the doorstep of Scott Jackson, who had been identified as Bryan's boyfriend. Aside from the fact that investigators usually start with suspects closest to the victim, it had also been determined that Bryan had been pregnant at the time of her death. Jackson, a dental student, only hesitated a moment before implicating fellow dental student Alonzo Walling as Bryan's murderer. Within twenty-four hours, both men were in custody.

Over the course of the next few days, as Pearl Bryan's body was moved to Greencastle's Forest Hill Cemetery to lie in state pending recovery of her head, police began to piece together the events surrounding her death. It seems that while Jackson's original plan was to force Bryan to have an abortion, that quickly dissolved and Jackson made the decision to kill her. Walling claimed that he did not participate in the actual murder, but that he knew of Jackson's plan and did nothing to stop it from happening. Both men were convicted of first-degree murder and sentenced to death for their crimes. They went to the gallows together on March 20, 1897, and were hanged in the front yard of the Newport Courthouse. To the very end, the one thing Jackson and Walling refused to talk about was the location of Bryan's head. After the executions, Bryan's family finally had to accept that Pearl's head was never going to be found and they reluctantly buried their daughter. To this day, its location has never been determined.

Popular ghostlore holds that when someone passes away missing a limb, or in this case a head, that the spirit will return to Earth in an attempt to locate the missing body part. If that is true, it would explain why the ghostly form of a headless woman is sometimes seen floating among the tombstones at Forest Hill Cemetery. Some say that it's the ghost of Pearl Bryan, still searching for her head. In a strange attempt to help poor Pearl, visitors to her grave place pennies, heads-up, on the tombstone. That way, some say, Pearl Bryan will at least have a head come Judgment Day.

Over the years many have visited Pearl's gravesite having heard of the tragic story. People have taken away small chips from her grave markers as mementos. Today, there is nothing left of the marker but the base.

Honk Three Times and She'll Come A-Running

Spanning the Little Walnut Creek at only eighty feet in length, the Edna Collings Bridge quickly became known as the "baby" of all Putnam County covered bridges when Charles Hendrix constructed it in 1922. Still, the bridge's isolated location along County Road 450 North made it the ideal spot for youngsters to jump into the cool water below for a refreshing swim.

Shortly after the bridge opened, a young girl whose name has been lost (although she is often mistakenly referred to as "Edna") made the water below the bridge her own personal swimming hole. She loved to swim so much that her parents often dropped her off at the bridge and let her play in the water while they ran errands. When they were done, the parents would drive up onto the bridge, turn the car off, and then honk the horn three times to let the girl

know they were there and it was time to go. Once she heard the horn, the girl would scamper up the embankment and jump in the car.

One day, though, the parents pulled onto the bridge and turned the car off as they had done so many times before. They honked the horn three times and then waited for their daughter to come running up to the car. After waiting several minutes with no sign of their daughter, the parents got out of the car and walked over to the edge of the bridge. Looking down into the water, they came across a horrible sight: their daughter floating facedown in the water. Tragically, the young girl had accidentally drowned while playing in the water.

It is said that tragic events often leave their imprint on an area. Perhaps that's why the Edna Collings Bridge has come to be known as haunted. Many will tell you that the events that unfolded on the bridge that day resulted in that young girl's ghost becoming trapped here on Earth. They say that if you go out to the bridge, turn your car off, and honk your horn three times, that the ghost of the young girl will mistake you for her parents calling her and will come walking towards your car. And if you let her, she just might climb inside the car with you, eager to finally leave the bridge for good.

Never Borrow One of James Whitcomb's Books without Asking

I am a book lover and as such, I have amassed an enormous personal library. In fact, my paranormal library alone is bulging with well over nine hundred volumes. When it comes to my books, while I encourage everyone to borrow and enjoy them, it annoys me to no end when I find that one of my prized volumes has walked off or someone has simply neglected to tell me that they borrowed one. That's why, when I came across the ghost story concerning the Whitcomb Collection at the DePauw University Library, I couldn't help but smile.

When he was alive, Indiana governor James Whitcomb was known far and wide for being a bibliophile. In fact, while he was alive, Whitcomb took great pride in acquiring some extremely rare volumes to add to his personal library. When he passed away in

1852, Whitcomb had made a special request in his will to ensure that his library remained intact to be enjoyed for years to come. He willed it to the Indiana Asbury University. The university gladly accepted the donation and a short time later, the Whitcomb Collection took up residence among the library stacks. Shortly after that, some say that Whitcomb's ghost moved in to the library. His ghost was sometimes reported near the Whitcomb Collection, as if he was keeping an eye on his books.

In 1884, the university changed its name to DePauw University, after businessman Washington C. DePauw, who had been making huge contributions to the university for the previous decade. But nothing changed for the Whitcomb Collection. Whitcomb's ghost was still reported lurking in the library, keeping an eye on his prized books. That is, until one day when a student borrowed (some say stole) a rare copy of James Macpherson's *The Poems of Ossian*.

The day after the student removed the Macpherson book from the library, the badly shaken boy returned it. In a trembling voice, he stated the previous evening, after retiring for the night, he awoke to find the ghost of James Whitcomb standing in his room. After remaining there in silence for what seemed like an eternity, Whitcomb's ghost suddenly began crying out "Ossian! Who stole the Ossian?" before simply vanishing.

The library staff wasn't entirely convinced of the boy's story. Still, they decided that the entire Whitcomb Collection needed to be placed under lock and key. This is how it resides to this day, making it virtually impossible for anyone to make off with a book. But that apparently hasn't stopped the ghost of James Whitcomb from making an appearance in the library every once in awhile, just to keep an eye on things and make sure all his books are safe and sound.

Bibliography

Books

Baker, Ronald L. *Hoosier Folk Legends*. Bloomington: Indiana University Press, 1984.

Baker, Tom, and Jonathan Titchenal. *Haunted Indianapolis and Other Indiana Ghost Stories*. Atglen, PA: Schiffer Publishing, 2007.

Belanger, Jeff. *Encyclopedia of Haunted Places: Ghostly Locales from around the World*. Franklin Lakes, NJ: Career Press, 2009.

———. *The Ghost Files*. Franklin Lakes, NJ: Career Press, 2007.

Bodenhamer, David J., and Robert G. Barrows, eds. *The Encyclopedia of Indianapolis*. Indianapolis: Indiana University Press, 1994.

Cavinder, Fred D. *Amazing Tales from Indiana*. Bloomington: Indiana University Press, 1990.

———. *More Amazing Tales from Indiana*. Bloomington: Indiana University Press, 2003.

———. *The Indiana Book of Records, Firsts, and Fascinating Facts*. Bloomington: Indiana University Press, 1985.

Davis, Dorothy Salvo. *Haunted Tales from the Region: Ghosts of Indiana's South Shore*. Charleston, SC: Haunted America, 2010.

Davis, Dorothy Salvo, and W. C. Madden. *Haunted Lafayette*. Charleston, SC: Haunted America, 2009.

Dean, John. *House of Evil: The Indiana Torture Slaying*. New York: St. Martin's Press, 2008.

Hauck, Dennis William. *Haunted Places: The National Directory*. New York: Penguin Books, 2002.

Hensley, Douglas. *Hell's Gate: Terror at Bobby Mackey's Music World*. Jacksonville, FL: Audio Books Plus, 1993.

Kartman, Ben, and Leonard Brown, eds. *Disaster!* Freeport, NY: Books for Libraries Press, 1948.

Kobrowski, Nicole R. *Encyclopedia of Haunted Indiana*. Westfield, IN: Unseen Press, 2009.

———. *Haunted Backroads: Central Indiana and Other Stories*. Westfield, IN: Unseen Press, 2009.

MacRorie, K. T. *Hoosier Hauntings*. Grand Rapids: Thunder Bay Press, 1997.

Meier, Nellie Simmons. *Lions' Paws: The Story of Famous Hands*. New York: Barrows Mussey, 1937.

Meriman, Mark. *Haunted Indiana*. Holt, MI: Thunder Bay Press, 1998.

———. *Haunted Indiana 2*. Holt, MI: Thunder Bay Press, 1999.

———. *Haunted Indiana 3*. Holt, MI: Thunder Bay Press, 2003.

———. *Haunted Indiana 4*. Holt, MI: Thunder Bay Press, 2005.

———. *Haunted Travels of Indiana*. Holt, MI: Thunder Bay Press, 2010.

Meriman, Mark, James Willis, and Troy Taylor. *Weird Ohio*. New York: Sterling Publishing, 2008.

Newton, Michael. *Strange Indiana Monsters*. Atglen, PA: Schiffer Publishing, 2006.

Norman, Michael, and Beth Scott. *Haunted America*. New York: Tom Doherty Associates, 1994.

———. *Historic Haunted America*. New York: Tom Doherty Associates, 1995.

Ogden, Tom. *The Complete Idiot's Guide to Ghosts and Hauntings*. Indianapolis: MacMillan USA, 1999.

Osborne, Stephen. *South Bend Ghosts*. Atglen, PA: Schiffer Publishing, 2009.

Pohlen, Jerome. *Oddball Indiana: A Guide to Some Really Strange Places*. Chicago: Chicago Review Press, 2002.

Sankowsky, Lorri, and Keri Young. *Ghost Hunter's Guide to Indianapolis*. Gretna, LA: Pelican Publishing, 2008.

Scott, Beth, and Michael Norman. *Haunted Heartland*. New York: Barnes and Noble, 1985.

Thay, Edrick. *Ghost Stories of Indiana*. Edmonton, AB: Lone Star Publishing, 2001.

Tucker, Elizabeth. *Haunted Halls: Ghostlore of American College Campuses*. Jackson: University Press of Mississippi, 2007.

Willis, Wanda Lou. *Haunted Hoosier Trails*. Cincinnati: Clerisy Press, 2002.

———. *More Haunted Hoosier Trails*. Cincinnati: Clerisy Press, 2004.

Wlodarski, Robert James, and Anne Powell Wlodarski. *Dinner and Spirits*. Lincoln, NE: iUniverse.com, 2001.

Wolfsie, Dick. *Indiana Curiosities*. Guilford, CT: Global Pequot Press, 2003.

Online Sources

"1963 Coliseum Explosion Killed 74." *Indystar.com*. Retrieved 23 April 2011. www2.indystar.com/library/factfiles/accidents/history/coliseum _explosion/coliseum.html.

"About Elkhart Civic Theatre." *Elkhart Civic Theatre*. Retrieved 4 March 2011. www.elkhartcivictheatre.org/about.asp.

Bibliography

"ARCH Tour Unveils Haunted Fort Wayne." *Fort Wayne Reader*. Retrieved 18 January 2011. www.fortwaynereader.com/story.php?uid = 603.

"Alice Gray, Woman Of The Dunes." *Chesterton Tribune*. Retrieved 3 March 2011. http://chestertontribune.com/Local%20History/alice_gray.htm.

"Barbee Hotel & Restaurant." *Barbee Hotel Restaurant and Bar*. Retrieved 24 March 2011. www.barbeehotel.com.

"Charles Sweeney vs. State of Indiana." *In.gov.com*. Retrieved 21 February 2011. www.in.gov/judiciary/opinions/pdf/04230801lmb.pdf.

"Christy Woods." *Ball State University*. Retrieved 7 March 2011. www.bsu.edu/map/bldngs/woods.

"Cold Spots: The Bristol Opera House." *Dread Central*. Retrieved 4 March 2011. www.dreadcentral.com/news/37853/cold-spots-the-bristol-opera-house.

"Cry-Woman's Bridge." *American Hauntings*. Retrieved 7 February 2011. www.prairieghosts.com/crywoman.html.

"Frances Slocum State Forest." *StateParks.com*. Retrieved 25 March 2011.www.stateparks.com/frances_slocum.html.

"Frances Slocum State Forest Trail Map." *Pickatrail*. Retrieved 18 March 2011. www.pickatrail.com/sun/f/america/forest/frances_slocum_state _forest_miami_indiana/map.html.

"From Vaudeville to Film, the Strand Has Staged It All." *Kpcnews.net*. Retrieved 9 March 2011. www.kpcnews.net/mainstreet/strand.htm.

"George and Nellie Meier Collection." *Indiana Historical Society*. Retrieved 27 January 2011. www.indianahistory.org/our-collections/collection-guides/george-and-nellie-meier-collection-ca-1900-1930s.pdf.

"Ghost Hunters Descend on Willard." *Courierpress.com*. Retrieved 2 March 2011. www.courierpress.com/news/2007/oct/22/ghost-hunters-descend-on-willard.

"Ghosts Reveal Hannah's House Secret." *Ghost Eyes: Most Haunted Places in America*. Retrieved 17 March 2011. www.ghosteyes.com/ghosts-reveal-hannahs-house-secret.

"Going Out in Style." *Douglas Keister Historic Architectural Photography*. Retrieved 12 April 2011. www.douglaskeister.com/going/detail.np/detail-52.html.

"Great Circus Train Wreck of 1918." *HammondIndiana.com*. Retrieved 21 February 2011. www.hammondindiana.com/history/circus.htm.

"Gypsy Graveyard." *Lowell Public Library*. Retrieved 12 May 2011. www.lowellpl.lib.in.us/gypsy.htm.

"Haunted Tour Features Elliott, Shively." *Bsudailynews.com*. Retrieved 5 February 2011. www.bsudailynews.com/2.14295/haunted-tour-features-elliott-shively-1.2008348.

"Indiana State University Archives: Cromwell Hall." *Indiana State University Cunningham Memorial Library*. Retrieved 8 February 2011. http://library .indstate.edu/archives/exhibits/architecture/CromwellHall.htm.

"French Lick Springs Hotel." *Indiana Paranormal*. Retrieved 4 March 2011. http://indianaparanormal.com/frenchlick.html.

"Ivanhoe, Indiana—1918." *Danger Ahead! Historic Railway Disasters.* Retrieved 21 February 2011. http://danger-ahead.railfan.net/gallery/ivanhoe_1918.html.

"ISU Legend Doesn't Hold Up to Truth." *Indiana Statesman.* Retrieved 8 February 2011. www.indianastatesman.com/news/isu-legend-doesn-t-hold-up-to-truth-1.1728929.

"Legend of Moody's Light." *Ghostvillage.com.* Retrieved 27 April 2011. www.ghostvillage.com/ghostcommunity/index.php?showtopic = 663.

"Legend of White Lick Creek Bridge." *About.com Indianapolis.* Retrieved 28 January 2011. http://indianapolis.about.com/od/landmarkslegends/a/HauntedBridge.htm.

Library Ghost. Retrieved 1 March 2011. www.libraryghost.com.

Mounds State Park. Retrieved 8 March 2011. www.moundsstatepark.org.

"New Bridge At Devil's Hollow." *Huntertown Historical Society.* Retrieved 21 February 2011. www.huntertownhistoricalsoc.org/Misc_Articles/new_bridge_at_devil.htm.

"Pearl Bryan Murder." *RootsWeb.* Retrieved 19 January 2011. www.rootsweb.ancestry.com/ ~ kycampbe/piecespearlbryan.htm.

"Purdue Airport Recognized as Aviation Historical Site." *Purdue University News Service.* Retrieved 9 May 2011. http://news.uns.purdue.edu/html3month/2005/050615.Petrin.airport.html.

Saint Joseph's College. Retrieved 9 February 2011. www.saintjoe.edu.

"Scare Yourself Silly: Haunted Houses In Indiana." *FunCityFinder.com.* Retrieved 24 March 2011. http://indianapolis-indiana.funcityfinder.com/2009/07/28/haunted-houses.

"Seven Pillars." *Miami County Indiana.* Retrieved 3 March 2001. www.miamicountyin.gov/SevenPillars.htm.

Slippery Noodle Inn. Retrieved 18 February 2011. www.slipperynoodle.com.

"Vernon Twp. Businesses." *Fortville-Vernon Township Public Library.* Retrieved 19 February 2011. www.fortville.lib.in.us/Genealogy/VernonTwpBusiness/tabid/712/Default.aspx.

"Wheeler-Stokely Mansion." *National Park Service.* Retrieved 7 March 2011. www.nps.gov/nr/travel/indianapolis/wsmansion.htm.

The Willard. Retrieved 3 February 2011. www.thewillard.com.

"Willard Library GhostCams." *WillardGhost.com.* Retrieved 1 March 2011. www.willardghost.com/?content = ghostcams.

Acknowledgments

I'D LIKE TO THANK THE FOLLOWING PEOPLE FOR THEIR CONTRIBUTIONS: Troy Taylor, my Invisible Friend, for recommending me to Stackpole Books and, more importantly, for working so hard to ensure the paranormal community still maintains a shred of its dignity; Kyle Weaver, for being one of the more laid-back editors I have ever had the pleasure to work with; Courtney, for making everything old seem new again; my sister, donna (yes, that's a lowercase "d"), for introducing me to Barnabas Collins and Carl Kolchak; Carol and Steve Flee, for keeping their eyes on the road while I wrote; Ernie, Maddy, and Bailey, for keeping me company during those long nights of writing; Khashoggi, for letting me know when bad weather was approaching; Mark and Mark, for being the first people to trust me in Indiana; Julie Black, Janine Bourdo, Wendy Cywinski, Mark DeLong, Roger Ganley, and Samantha Nicholson, for following me down the dark and spooky roads that would become the basis for this book; Ronald L. Baker, author of *Hoosier Folk Tales*, whom I've never met, but whose book was a huge inspiration to me; Mike and Kris Baker, the founders of the world's only official James A. Willis Fan Club and the first people to publicly declare me Weird Willis; everyone at The Ghosts of Ohio, for encouraging me to write this book and for begging to come on some of the road trips; and everyone who shared their Indiana ghost stories with me, even if you didn't think I was going to believe them.

Thanks also to you—yes, you!—the dashing sir or madam holding a copy of *Haunted Indiana* and reading these very words. Thank you for allowing me the opportunity to share some of my stories with you.

And saving the best for last, I'd like to thank my wife Stephanie, who knew from the start I was a strange and spooky guy and still decided to marry me. Thank you, Steph, for all those times when your love and support were the only things that kept me going. It will take a lifetime to try and repay you for all you've done for me . . . but I'm sure gonna have fun trying!

About The Author

Fueled by a steady childhood diet of Boo Berry cereal, *Creepy* magazine, and late-night Vincent Price movies, author and paranormal researcher James A. Willis developed a taste for the unexplained at an early age and quickly began seeking out all things strange and spooky. When he wasn't trying to coax the boogeyman out from under his bed for a photo shoot, Willis pondered such eternal questions as . . . What happens to us when we die? Is there life on other planets? And what possesses someone to decorate their house with 1,001 milk jugs?

In 1999, after spending more than fifteen years chasing after ghosts and visiting crybaby bridges, Willis moved to Ohio and founded The Ghosts of Ohio (ghostsofohio.org), a nationally recognized paranormal research organization. The organization has grown to three divisions throughout the state: Columbus, Cleveland, and Cincinnati.

In 2004, in what seemed to be destiny, Mark Moran and Mark Sceurman, the architects of the Weird U.S. series of books, approached Willis and asked him to contribute to their latest volume, *Weird U.S.* To date, Willis has been involved with six books in the Weird U.S. series, including *Weird Indiana*, *Weird Ohio*, and

Weird Encounters. Willis's unique and offbeat writing style was officially recognized in 2006 with his induction into the Grand Order of Weird Writers.

In addition, Willis has been a contributing author to several books in the Armchair Reader series, including *Weird, Scary & Unusual* and *Armchair Reader Goes Hollywood*.

Willis has been featured in more than fifty media sources, including CNN, *USA Today, Columbus Business First, Midwest Living,* the *Canadian Press,* and even the *Kuwait Times*. He is also currently a contributing author to *Mysteries Magazine*.

Willis resides in Columbus, Ohio, with his wife and daughter, a parrot who loves the music of Queen, and three narcoleptic cats.

Also Available in the

Haunted Series

Haunted Illinois
by Troy Taylor
978-0-8117-3499-8

The mysterious and often violent history of Illinois has
made the state a haven for restless spirits. This volume
explores the supernatural side of the Prairie State, with
stories on the horrors of an old slave house, the
numerous spirits of Alton's McPike Mansion, the
cemetery where the dead walk, the Spring Valley
Vampire, the ghosts of the Bartonville Asylum,
Chicago's famous Resurrection Mary, and the spirit
world of Abraham Lincoln.

WWW.STACKPOLEBOOKS.COM
1-800-732-3669

Also Available in the

Haunted Series

Haunted Kentucky
by Alan Brown
978-0-8117-3584-1

Horses graze peacefully in the bucolic pastures of the
Bluegrass State, but this surface beauty is offset by a violent
past of Indian wars and Civil War battles. In addition to the
tragic spirits from these conflicts, this volume includes
stories about the headless ghost of Old Fort Herrod, the
vanishing hitchhiker of Meshack Road, the Great Meat
Storm of 1876, and the sinister witch's grave at Pilot's Knob
Cemetery. A host of strange creatures also wander the state,
among them Goat Man, Lizard Man, and the
Herrington Lake Monster.

WWW.STACKPOLEBOOKS.COM
1-800-732-3669

Other Titles in the
Haunted Series